P9-DXM-628

You're Reading the WRONG WAY!

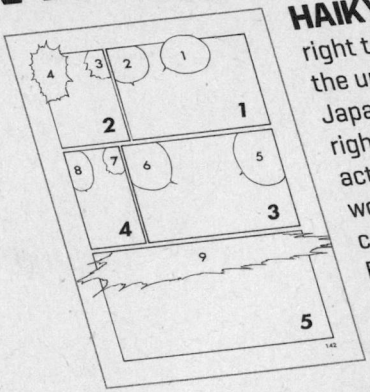

HAIKYU!! reads from right to left, starting in the upper-right corner. Japanese is read from right to left, meaning that action, sound effects and word-balloon order are completely reversed from English order.

A SEASON OF DRAMA.
A TALE OF A LIFETIME!

SLAM DUNK

BY TAKEHIKO INOUE
CREATOR OF
VAGABOND AND *REAL*
MANGA SERIES
ON SALE NOW

SHONEN JUMP
www.shonenjump.com

© 1990–2008 Takehiko Inoue and I.T. Planning, Inc.

RATED T FOR TEEN
ratings.viz.com

viz media
www.viz.com

EDITOR'S NOTES

The English edition of Haikyu!! maintains the honorifics used in the original Japanese version. For those of you who are new to these terms, here's a brief explanation to help with your reading experience!

When saying someone's name in Japanese, a suffix is often attached to indicate how familiar the speaker is with the person. Some are more polite and respectful, while others are endearing.

1. ***-kun*** is often used for young men or boys, usually someone you are familiar with.

2. ***-chan*** is used for young children and can be used as a term of endearment.

3. ***-san*** is used for someone you respect or are not close to, or to be polite.

4. ***Senpai*** is used for someone who is older than you or in a higher position or grade in school.

5. ***Kohai*** is used for someone who is younger than you or in a lower position or grade in school.

6. ***Sensei*** means teacher.

HAIKYU!! VOL 1: HINATA AND KAGEYAMA (END)

"THE BALL CAME!"
"THE BALL CAME, KAGEYAMA!!"
?
??
"I'M HERE!!"
...
I...
?!
BUH ?!
TWITCH
SILENCE
...THEN I WILL!
I'M JEALOUS OF YOUR ATHLETICISM!
HUH?!
I'LL MAKE USE OF EVERYTHING YOU'VE GOT!
?!
WHAT ?
IF YOU WON'T USE IT...
BWAAAH?!
WATCHING YOU WASTE IT ALL THE TIME TICKS ME OFF!!

!
THERE'S NO WAY YOU CAN'T SEE YOUR TEAMMATES TOO!
YOU HAVE THE SKILL. YOU HAVE THE TALENT. YOU HAVE MORE THAN ENOUGH ENTHUSIASM ...
BUT MOST IMPORTANTLY... YOU HAVE THE INCREDIBLE VISION TO SEE EVERYTHING AROUND YOU.
GLANCE
?!
HOW?! SOMEHOW, SOME WAY...
GOOOONG
...
??
?
"CAN'T YOU SOMEHOW FIND SOME WAY TO TAKE ADVANTAGE OF THAT IN WHATEVER THE BEST WAY IS?!"

I DUNNO, UM...
TAKE HINATA'S UNIQUE SKILL SET, HIS...HIS "HINATA-NESS"...
AND, YOU KNOW... UMM... DO...DO MORE... UH...
YOU CAN DO IT, SUGA-SAN!
Spit it out!
Spit it out, man!
CAN'T YOU SOMEHOW FIND SOME WAY TO TAKE ADVANTAGE OF THAT IN WHATEVER THE BEST WAY IS?!
SEE, UM...
?
I'M A SETTER, LIKE YOU ARE.
WATCHING YOU IN LAST YEAR'S GAME...I WAS STUPEFIED.
YOUR EXACTING BALL CONTROL! YOUR INCREDIBLE INSTINCTS!
BUT MOST OF ALL...
YOUR BROAD VISION AND DECISIVENESS THAT LET YOU DISSECT THE OPPONENT'S MOVES AND DETERMINE RIGHT WHERE THEY'D BLOCK!
ALL OF THAT...
...IS STUFF I CAN'T DO.
WHA?! N-NO WAY, SUGA-SAN! YOU'RE--
TANAKA.
TRY JUST LISTENING FOR ONCE.
...

HINATA IS EXCEPTIONALLY MOBILE. HE'S FAST, HAS GOOD REFLEXES, AND HE CAN JUMP.
WITH TIME AND PRACTICE, HE SHOULD BE ABLE TO GET USED TO--
YEAH, BUT!
...?
OH!
UMMM ...
UM...
DON'T YOU THINK THE WAY YOU'RE SETTING NOW...
...IS HINDERING HINATA'S BEST WEAPON--HIS SPEED?
!
BUT TALENT-WISE, HE HAS POTENTIAL!
!
THAT'S NOT WHAT HE SAID.
AW, SHUCKS. A GREAT TALENT? TH-THAT'S TOO MUCH...
HINATA IS A COMPLETE NEWBIE. HE HAS NO EXPERIENCE OR SKILL.
HE'S NOT LIKE THE ELITE HITTERS YOU HAD IN MIDDLE SCHOOL WHO COULD BARELY KEEP UP WITH YOU.
SUGAWARA-SAN?!
...
WITH YOUR SKILL, DON'T YOU THINK YOU COULD, UH...
?

THIS AIN'T FISHIN', FLOUNDER !!
YES! I TOUCHED IT--APH!!
FLUMP
NET FAULT!

WHIFF
SWISH
HNGH !!
AHA HA! SWING AN' A MISS!

ZING
NFF!!

KAGEYAMA.
THAT'S NOT THE IMPORTANT PART!!
"WOOSH," OR "ZOOM," WHICH IS IT?!
C'MON, YOU'RE FAST! CAN'T YOU, I DUNNO, COME IN MORE LIKE...WOOSH! YOU KNOW... ZOOM!
SWISH

GAH! I CAN'T GET THE TIMING DOWN AT ALL!
WHEEZE
HUFF

AT THIS RATE...
YOU'RE JUST REPEATING MIDDLE SCHOOL ALL OVER AGAIN.

TMP
?

ZIP
MWHAAA ?!
JU--
NGRRR!
HNN!
WHIFF
WHIFF
WSH
THERE IT IS. THE ROYAL SET.
TCH !!
...
...
WHAT WERE YOU DOING?!
MOVE FA--
!!
TU
DINK
...
IT'S THAT FAST?
BUH?

DUN
SET THAT BALL WHEREVER YOU WANT!
ALL RIGHT! BRING IT ON!
BOING
BOING
...
BOFF
TMP
OKAY! SO HE'S GONNA SET IT ON THE RIGHT!
TSUKKI, GOOD LUCK!
WE HAVEN'T COME UP WITH ANY HAND SIGNALS YET.
POINT POINT
THIS'LL DO FOR NOW...
NOD NOD NOD
NEXT I RUN OVER TO THE RIGHT AND...
TMP
GOOD RECEIVE!
BMP
HIS SERVES ARE SOFTER THAN AUNTIE YOSHIDA'S (FROM THE HOUSEWIVES' CLUB) ARE.
THERE!

...TO RUN UP AND HIT MY SET. GOT IT?
I WANT YOU TO USE EVERY LAST OUNCE OF YOUR SPEED AND REFLEXES...
WE GO AROUND.
IF WE CAN'T GO THROUGH...
LISTEN.
WE'RE GONNA GIVE IT A TRY ANYWAY!
...!
LIAR!! YOU SO DID NOT GET THAT!!
...? GOT IT!!
...
WAS THAT SUPPOSED TO BE AN EXPLANATION FOR A QUICK SET?!
DWAH ?!
WITH HINATA'S SPEED AND REFLEXES, HE SHOULD BE ABLE TO HIT A FASTER SET.
ALL RIIIIGHT !!
WSH
WSH
SERVER UP!!
BRING IT ON!!
I WASN'T DEPRESSED!
?
WHAT'S GOTTEN INTO YOU, ANYWAY? YOU WERE DEPRESSED AS HECK A MINUTE AGO.
WHRL
YES YOU WERE, YOU LIAR!!

?!
...?
DUN
THAT'S WHAT A SETTER IS FOR.

...
WHEN-EVER YOU GET THE BALL...
...SEND IT TO ME!!
I'LL JUMP TO WHEREVER IT IS!
AND I'LL HIT IT, NO MATTER WHAT KIND OF SET IT IS!
SO ...
...
TMP
TMP
?
BREAKING DOWN THE WALL SO THE HITTERS CAN GET THROUGH.
...

I WANT TO STAY OUT ON THE COURT!
...
IF YOU WANNA BE A DEFENSE-ONLY LIBERO, THAT'S ONE THING. BUT A HITTER? NO.
OR DO YOU THINK YOU CAN WILL YOURSELF A FOOT TALLER?
NICE THOUGHTS AND SENTIMENT MEAN NOTHING IN REALITY.
THAT'S A NICE THOUGHT, BUT THERE ISN'T ANYTHING YOU CAN DO.

...!
KAGEYAMA.
THAT'S ENOUGH. GO SIT ON THE BENCH.
...
SHO-CHAN.
WE SHOULD LINE UP.
NO. I DON'T WANNA GO JUST YET.
KARASUNO HIGH SCHOOL
SO I CAN STAY OUT ON THE COURT AS LONG AS I CAN!

HE'S LIKE...
...A LITTLE GIANT!!
WHEN I HEARD THAT...
...I WANTED TO BE LIKE THAT TOO.
SCHOOL
KARASUNO HIGH SCHOOL
THIS IS THE ONLY BODY I'VE GOT.
I WANNA KEEP TRYING...
I WANNA KEEP WINNING ...
SO YEAH...
BEING SHORT IS A DISADVANTAGE.
I MIGHT NOT BE CUT OUT FOR THIS.
BUT I DON'T CARE. THAT DOESN'T MATTER TO ME.

NAB
...
...AND HERE IN HIGH SCHOOL TOO...
YEAH... BACK IN MIDDLE SCHOOL ...
SEE, SOME PEOPLE JUST AREN'T CUT OUT FOR SOME THINGS.
I STILL GET STOPPED BY BLOCKERS EVERY TIME.
NO MATTER WHAT I DO...
HOW FAST I RUN...
HOW HIGH I JUMP...
BUT...
NO MATTER HOW HIGH I JUMP, IT DOESN'T DO ANYTHING TO MAKE UP FOR THAT ABSOLUTE GAP IN HEIGHT.
...IS A SPORT WHERE HEIGHT IS REALLY IMPORTANT.
VOLLEYBALL...

WHAT'S WRONG WITH YOU TODAY?! ALL THIS ACTING QUIET AND TIMID AND STUFF IS CREEPING ME OUT! QUIT IT!
POINT
SHUT UP.
...!!
IMPOSSIBLE?! THE KAGEYAMA JUST SAID THE WORD "IMPOSSIBLE"?! I DIDN'T THINK HE KNEW WHAT THAT MEANT!!
GLARE
IT'D BE IMPOSSIBLE FOR US TO PULL OFF A QUICK SET NOW.
WE'VE NEVER DONE ANY SERIOUS COMBO PRACTICE TOGETHER.
...SCARES ME DOWN TO THE BOTTOM OF MY SOUL.
YEAH. I AM. THE IDEA THAT NO ONE WILL BE THERE WHEN I PUT THE BALL UP...
...
YOU'RE TERRIFIED TO EVEN ATTEMPT A QUICK SET.
JUST WINGING IT AND TRYING YOUR VERY BEST ISN'T GOING TO WORK FOR EVERYTHING, Y'KNOW.
?
GEEZ, LOOK AT YOU, GETTING ALL TICKED OFF AGAIN.
SHUT UP! I'LL ZING ONE RIGHT PAST YOU NEXT TIME, JUST YOU WAIT!!
THE KING SURE ISN'T ACTING VERY ROYAL TODAY, IS HE.
SNAP

...BUT THERE'S NO DENYING THAT HE IS AN AMAZING TALENT.
RIGHT NOW HE'S UNFORTUNATELY MORE NOTICEABLE FOR HIS BAD ATTITUDE...
I'VE ONLY EVER SPIKED BALLS THAT GET TOSSED UP IN BIG, HIGH ARCS.
HUH? NOPE.
TOSS
THAT SUPER-FAST ATTACK YOU JUST DID!
WHAT'S THAT?
YOU TWO KNOW HOW TO DO A QUICK SET?!
STMP
STMP
ANY KIND! GOT IT?!
WHRL
BUT FROM NOW ON, I'LL HIT ANY KIND OF SET!
HUH? OH, THAT? I DON'T REMEMBER HOW I DID IT.
THEN THERE WAS THAT ONE YOU HIT IN THAT GAME WHERE YOUR SETTER POPPED IT UP IN THE WRONG DIRECTION!
BUT YOU JUST DID IT A SECOND AGO!
ARGH!
...

!
I'M HERE!!
ZIP
HE ONLY REACTED TO HINATA'S SHOUT AT THE LAST SECOND AND STILL MANAGED TO SET THE BALL WITH PINPOINT ACCURACY.
KAGEYAMA DEFINITELY LOOKED LIKE HE WAS ABOUT TO PUT THAT UP FOR TANAKA.

CHAPTER 7: Words from the Have-Nots

KOUSHI SUGAWARA

KARASUNO HIGH SCHOOL
CLASS 3-4

VOLLEYBALL CLUB
VICE CAPTAIN

POSITION: SETTER

HEIGHT: 5'9"
WEIGHT: 140 LBS.
(AS OF APRIL, 3RD YEAR OF HIGH SCHOOL)

BIRTHDAY: JUNE 13

FAVORITE FOOD:
SUPER-SPICY MAPO TOFU

CURRENT WORRY:
A LOT OF THE TEAM'S UNDERCLASSMEN ARE TALLER THAN HIM.

ABILITY PARAMETERS
(5-POINT SCALE)

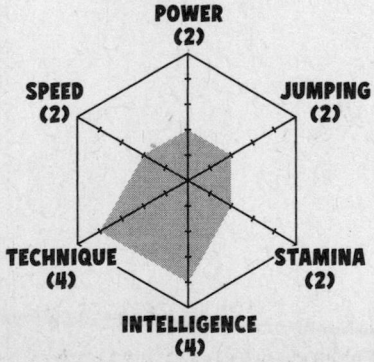

WHEN-EVER YOU GET THE BALL...
...SEND IT TO ME!!
KARASUNO HIGH SCHOOL

WHEW! THAT WAS CLOSE.
?!
THOUGHT I'D WHIFFED FOR A SECOND.
BLNK
SWISH
HNGH !!
DWAH ?!
WIFFLE
DOINK
THE BALL CAME, KAGEYAMA!! IT WAS THERE!!
WHAT THE HECK WAS THAT, ALL OF A SUDDEN?!
BDMP BDMP
I'LL JUMP TO WHEREVER IT IS!
AND I'LL HIT IT, NO MATTER WHAT KIND OF SET IT IS!
SO ...
I DON'T KNOW WHAT IT WAS LIKE FOR YOU IN MIDDLE SCHOOL, OKAY?!
ALL I KNOW IS THAT I'M SUPER GRATEFUL FOR ANY BALL THAT GETS PUT UP FOR ME!
!

ZIP
...!
I'M HERE!!
WHRL

THERE WAS NO ONE...
BUT...

TMP
TMP
FREE BALL!
TANAKA-SAN!
GOT IT!
?
IF YOU THINK THAT IF YOU JUST TRY REALLY HARD EVERYTHING WILL MAGICALLY WORK OUT, YOU HAVE ANOTHER THING COMING.
ENTHUSIASM AND GUTS AREN'T ENOUGH TO MAKE UP FOR BEING A FOOT TOO SHORT.
...?
TMP
TANAKA-SAN--
?!
KAGE-YAMA!!
TMP
WHO TO GIVE IT TO?
HINATA STILL CAN'T GO ONE-ON-ONE WITH TSUKISHIMA AND WIN.
TANAKA-SAN IS THE BETTER BET.
BRING IT!!!
GIVE IT TO ME!!
HERE HERE HEEERE!!

RIGHT NOW, THE BIGGER PROBLEM IS HOW TO GET ONE PAST YOU!
POINT
...
HA HA!
BFF!
...I'LL GO AFTER IT EVERY TIME--SO THAT DOESN'T MATTER ANYMORE.
IF THERE'S SOMEONE THERE TO SET THE BALL FOR ME...
...
THAT KIND OF PURE, EARNEST AND STRAIGHT-FORWARD ATTITUDE...
Y'KNOW ...
...MAKES ME SICK.
HN?
WHAT ELSE MATTERS RIGHT NOW BESIDES THAT?
AND PUT THE BALL UP FOR ME.
THEN YOU'RE GONNA GET TO BE THE OFFICIAL SETTER!
WE'RE GONNA BEAT TSUKISHIMA AND JOIN THE TEAM FOR REAL!

Y'KNOW, I'M GETTING REEEAL TIRED OF HEARIN' YOU TALK.
TANAKA.
...
...
...SCARES ME DOWN TO THE BOTTOM OF MY SOUL.
?
THE IDEA THAT NO ONE WILL BE THERE WHEN I PUT THE BALL UP...
YEAH.
I AM.
?
WAIT.
BUT THAT WAS ALL BACK IN MIDDLE SCHOOL, RIGHT?
...

KAGE-YAMA.
IT SAID, "WE AREN'T FOLLOWING YOU ANYMORE."
THAT ONE MISSED BALL WAS A STATEMENT ON THEIR PART...
IT WAS DELIB-ERATE REFUSAL.
...
UH-HUH. AND THANKS TO THAT GAME...
...YOU'RE TERRIFIED TO EVEN ATTEMPT A QUICK SET.
...
THAT'S ENOUGH.
GO SIT ON THE BENCH.

...
北川第一
...
COACH
HUFF
GET THERE IN TIME TO HIT MY SETS!!
MOVE FASTER !!
JUMP HIGHER !!
IF YOU WANT TO WIN...
...I PUT THE BALL UP...
...OUR OPPONENT'S MATCH POINT...
...AT THE END OF THE FIRST SET...
THEN ...
THAT WASN'T OUR FIRST BOTCHED COMBO-PLAY OF THE DAY.
BUT THAT ONE WASN'T AN ACCIDENT.
BUT THERE WAS NO ONE THERE TO HIT IT.
北川第一
2

!
...AND YOU GOT BENCHED.
...YOUR TYRANNY WENT TOO FAR...
AFTER ALL, DURING THAT FINALS MATCH ...
"MOVE FASTER!!"
BUT TO WIN, WE HAVE TO FIND A WAY AROUND THEIR BLOCKS!
AM I GOING TO LOSE HERE?
IS THIS REALLY WHERE IT ENDS?
NO! I'M NOT GOING TO LOSE! I'M GOING TO NATIONALS!
CUT IT OUT, MAN!
WHAT'S THE POINT IF WE CAN'T HIT 'EM?!
YOUR SETS ARE FREAKIN' IMPOS-SIBLE!!
NGH!

PEOPLE AT OTHER SCHOOLS STARTED CALLING HIM THAT BECAUSE HE INTIMIDATES THEM, RIGHT?
HUH? IT'S BECAUSE HE'S A SUPER-AMAZING ELITE PLAYER.
HA HA!
THERE ARE A LOT OF PEOPLE WHO THINK THAT'S IT.
?
DON'T YOU KNOW THE REASON HE'S CALLED THE KING?
WHAT.
HEY!! HOW COME YOU KEEP TRYING TO MESS WITH HIM?!
STMP
STMP
WHAT'S THAT ROYAL SET OR WHATEVER, AND WHY'S IT MATTER?!
THEY WERE CALLING HIM...
BY THE KING'S OWN TEAMMATES, IN FACT.
RUMOR HAS IT THAT IT BEGAN INSIDE KITAGAWA DAIICHI.
BUT IT WASN'T OTHER PLAYERS WHO STARTED CALLING HIM "THE KING OF THE COURT."
...
...BUT WHEN I WATCHED THAT GAME, I UNDERSTOOD WHY.
I'D HEARD THE RUMORS BEFORE-HAND, OF COURSE ...
A TYRANNICAL DICTATOR WHO ALWAYS HAD TO HAVE HIS WAY.
...A SELF-CENTERED KING.

DAICHI-SAN'S STRENGTH ISN'T ON OFFENSE. IT'S HIS STABLE, CONSISTENT RECEIVING.
HE'S A MONSTER ON DEFENSE.
GRR!
BA
YAMA-GUCHI.
LEAVE IT TO ME, TSUKKI!
GAK!
BAM
...IS AN EXTRA TWO YEARS OF EXPERIENCE AT RECEIVING ALL KINDS OF SERVES.
BUT WHAT I DO HAVE...
I DON'T HAVE ANY EYE-OPENING TALENTS LIKE YOU DO.
WERE YOU HOPING YOU COULD SCORE ON US A FEW TIMES IN A ROW?
?
...
DON'T YOU THINK IT'S ABOUT TIME FOR THE KING TO GET SERIOUS?
C'MON, YOUR MAJESTY!
!
!!
HN?!
WE AREN'T GOING TO BE AS EASY TO BREAK DOWN AS YOU THINK.

FLINCH
EEP!
ZWOOM
GO!
BAM
?!
FWIF
BUMP

I DON'T NEED TO USE ANY OF MY FAST ATTACKS.
TMP
?
I-I'M SORRY, TSUKKI!
TCH!
OOPS!!
BAP
OOF
IT'S OKAY!
FWEEP
YAMAGUCHI, IT'S THEIR TURN.
SHUT UP.
TATAM
TAM
BRING OUT THE KILLER SERVE!
KAGEYAMA DOES HAVE A REALLY MEAN JUMP SERVE.
ZIP
TIME FOR ME TO SCORE A BUNCH IN A ROW ON YOU.
GET 'EM!
TMP
TMP
I HAVE OTHER WAYS TO BEAT YOU.

G...
GIVE IT TO ME AGAIN!
I'LL SCORE THE NEXT TIME!
HE'S TALL, BUT THERE'S ONLY ONE OF HIM.
...
IF ONLY YOU WERE A MEASLY 12 INCHES TALLER. THEN YOU MIGHT'VE BEEN A SUPER-STAR!
I WAS REALLY SHOCKED WHEN I SAW THAT YESTERDAY. FOR A SHRIMP, YOU SURE CAN JUMP!
WHAP
...
DANG IT.
AWW!
!
SHOOT!
TANAKA MANAGES TO PUNCH IT THROUGH PRETTY OFTEN THOUGH.
THIS MAKES HOW MANY TIMES NOW?
STUFFED AGAIN.
THMP
C'MON, YOU TWO. I'M STUFFING YOU LIKE A TURKEY.
HE'S BETTER THAN I THOUGHT.
OH, RIIIGHT. IT TENDS TO LEAVE YOUR HITTER IN THE DUST TOO, DOESN'T IT.
WHY DON'T YOU BREAK OUT YOUR ROYAL SET? YOU KNOW, THE ONE THAT LEAVES YOUR OPPONENTS IN THE DUST?

WHAP
IT'S HERE TOO.
...BY THAT TALL, TALL WALL...
DOOM
AGAIN I'M BLOCKED...
LOOM
BAM

WOOSH
...HE'S NOT THE ONLY ONE!
Free ball!
TANAKA-SAN IS REALLY AWESOME, BUT...
BMP
HINATA!
THE BALL GETS SET FOR ME TOO!
YEAH!
TMP
TMP
SWIP
DMP
ALL RIGHT! HERE GOES MY FIRST SPIKE IN MY FIRST HIGH SCHOOL GAME!!
AND MY VERY FIRST SCORE!!
SWOOO
?!
YAMMER
02
01

BAM
!
HNNN ...
GRAAAAH !!
THMP
WHOA!
HE SMASHED ONE RIGHT THROUGH THAT BIG FIRST YEAR!
TMP
TA-TMP
FRONT! FRONT!
LOOKS LIKE GETTING TANAKA RILED UP MIGHT NOT HAVE BEEN THE BEST PLAN.
TCH!
Shut up!!
PUT YOUR SHIRT BACK ON!
THAT'S ONLY ONE POINT!
BOO!
BOO!
YEEEEAAAAH!!! NOOOOOO!!!
YOU'RE OVER-DOING IT!
TANAKA, SHUT UP!!
WOOOW! THAT WAS EVEN STRONGER THAN USUAL!

BAM! BAM! BAM! BAM!
KITA ICHI !!
MIDDLE SCHOOL INTERSCHOLASTIC SPORTS TOURNAMENT
KITA ICHI !!
BAM! BAM!
KITA ICHI !!
*JERSEY: KOUSEN ACADEMY
光仙学園
PREFECTURAL QUALIFIERS--FINALS
CHAPTER 6: Middle School Story
SET UP A QUICK ATTACK SO FAST THEIR BLOCKING CAN'T KEEP UP.
I NEED TO BE FASTER...
THEIR BLOCKING IS TOUGH. I HAVE TO FIND SOME WAY PAST IT.
CRUD!
...
COACH
TCH!
...
MOVE FASTER!!
GOTTA JUMP HIGHER!
GOTTA MOVE FASTER!

DAICHI SAWAMURA

KARASUNO HIGH SCHOOL
CLASS 3-4

VOLLEYBALL CLUB CAPTAIN

POSITION: WING SPIKER

HEIGHT: 5'10"
WEIGHT: 154 LBS.
(AS OF APRIL, 3RD YEAR IN HIGH SCHOOL)

BIRTHDAY: DECEMBER 31

FAVORITE FOOD:
SOY-SAUCE RAMEN

CURRENT WORRY:
HE IS BEING PLAGUED BY NIGHTMARES OF THE VICE PRINCIPAL'S TOUPEE FLYING OFF OVER AND OVER AGAIN.

ABILITY PARAMETERS
(5-POINT SCALE)

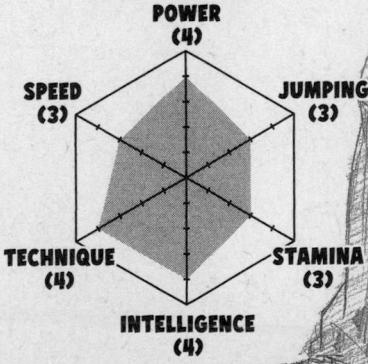

?!
OH MY GAWSH, DID YOU HEAR THAT? ALL THOSE THINGS HE SAID!
Tee hee hee!
GOOD-NESS, THAT TSUKI-SHIMA BRAT.
I GUESS WE'RE JUST GONNA HAFTA...
3-ON-3 MATCH...
...GIVE 'IM THE THRASHING OF HIS LIFE!!
FWEEP
SET 1, GAME START.

ER...
AHEM!!

BUT I WON'T GO EASY ON YOU. OKAY?
...

RELAX, RELAX. TANAKA IS WAY BETTER THAN ME ON OFFENSE.
HA HA HA!
TMP
TMP

GAH!! TSUKKI, SHH!! THEY CAN HEAR YOU!
SHHH!
TMP
WOW. TSUKISHIMA, YOU HAVE ONE SPECTACULARLY WARPED PERSONALITY.
AND I'D APPRECIATE IT IF THEY'D LOSE THEIR COOL FOR ME TOO.
THAT'S THE POINT. I WANT THEM TO HEAR ME.

AHEM! I MEAN, WHO SHOULD WE CONTAIN FIRST, TANAKA-SAN OR THE SHRIMP?
HEY, CAPTAIN. WHO SHOULD WE CRUSH...

I AM VERY MUCH LOOKING FORWARD TO WATCHING HIS MAJESTY, THE KING, LOSE.
OH, AND ...

...

PSST! PSST!

WHAT I ESPECIALLY WANT TO SEE...
...IS HOW THE LONELY, SOLITARY KING DOES, NOW THAT ALL HIS RETAINERS HAVE ABANDONED HIM.

SATURDAY
THE NEXT DAY...
...
THE DAY OF THE 3-ON-3 GAME
SILENCE
C'MON, LOOK! SHE'S SUPER PRETTY!
GLANCE
GLANCE
THERE'S A PRETTY GIRL! HEY, DO YOU THINK SHE'S OUR MANAGER?
OVER THERE!
LOOK!
TP
TP
WHA?! CAPTAIN, YOU'RE GONNA PLAY?!
I'LL JOIN TSUKISHIMA AND YAMAGUCHI TO EVEN UP THE NUMBERS.
ALL RIGHT, GUYS. LET'S GET THIS STARTED!
GEEZ! WHAT'S WRONG WITH HIM? HE'S BEEN ACTING FUNNY SINCE YESTERDAY.

OH, WAIT. TOMORROW WE'RE OPPONENTS. RIGHT.
I'M LOOKING FORWARD TO WITNESSING HIS MAJESTY'S ROYAL SETTING IN PERSON.
...
TADASHI YAMAGUCHI
KARASUNO HIGH SCHOOL
1ST YEAR
MIDDLE BLOCKER (MB)
KEI TSUKISHIMA, CLASS 1-4.
AS OF TODAY, I'M YOUR NEW TEAMMATE.
KEI TSUKISHIMA
KARASUNO HIGH SCHOOL
1ST YEAR
VOLLEYBALL CLUB
MIDDLE BLOCKER (MB)
WHAT'S WRONG?
TSUKKI, WAIT UP!
STMP
...
STMP
STMP
STUPIDLY INTENSE PEOPLE WHO GET ALL WORKED UP OVER A DUMB GAME PISS ME OFF.
THE KING, THAT MIDGET... JUST LOOKING AT THEM IRRITATES ME.
AND YOU'RE A BIG FAT JERK TOO!!
SHUT UP.
...
LET'S CRUSH HIM GOOD IN TOMOR-ROW'S GAME!
GEEZ! WHO DOES THAT BIG FAT-MOUTHED JERK THINK HE IS?!
YOU DON'T HAVE TO TELL ME THAT!
GRR!

TOMORROW, I'M GONNA ZING ONE RIGHT PAST YOUR EAR!!
...
GLARE
OH...?
HOLD IT!
WHO ARE YOU ANYWAY?!
WHAT DO YOU MEAN, A DUMB GAME?!
ANYWAYS, SEE YOU TWO TOMORROW.
I MEAN EXACTLY WHAT I SAID.
...
YOU T-TRYIN' TO S-START SOMETHIN' ...?
W-W-WHAT ...
URK!
SKITTER SKITTER
I MEAN... IT'S JUST A DUMB GAME.
C'MON, WHAT'RE YOU GETTING ALL WORKED UP FOR?
TOMORROW, LET'S HAVE SOME FUN AND NOT STRESS OUT, OKAY?

?!
SHVR
?!

SHUT UP ABOUT ALL THAT KING STUFF ALREADY!

DON'T FORGET ME!
I'M HERE TOO!

WOOOH

WHAT THE HECK?! I HAVE NO CLUE WHAT ANY OF THIS IS ABOUT, BUT WHY AREN'T YOU SAYING ANYTHING TO THAT BIG JERK?
??
GET TICKED OFF AND RIP INTO THAT GUY WITH ALL YOUR SNARKY LITTLE UNNECESSARY COMMENTS, LIKE YOU ALWAYS DO! C'MON!
...
SWF
WHAT, RUNNING AWAY? LOOKS LIKE THE KING ISN'T ALL HE'S CRACKED UP TO BE.
!
TOSS
TOSS
WHO KNOWS? MAYBE TOMORROW...
...I MIGHT JUST HAPPEN TO BEAT HIS MAJESTY, THE KING--
TOSS
WE'RE DONE FOR TONIGHT.
?!
WHA?!
HEY!!
WSH

BUT...
RIGHT, RIGHT. IT'S BECAUSE THEY COULDN'T THAT THINGS TURNED OUT THE WAY THEY DID.
...!
?
I'M SURPRISED THE OTHER GUYS PUT UP WITH YOUR SELF-CENTERED SETTING LIKE THAT!
I WOULDN'T.
OH, WAIT!
...WHEN I PUT THE BALL UP...
?!
TSUKKI!
YANK

WHAT IS?
DON'T YOU EVER CALL E--
OH-HO! SO IT'S TRUE.
GRR
TWITCH
!
SUCH CONFI-DENCE!
HA HA!
I GUESS THAT'S A KING FOR YOU.
...IT PISSES YOU OFF.
THE RUMOR THAT SAYS WHEN YOU GET CALLED "THE KING OF THE COURT"...
MP TMP TMP
...
WHAT'RE YOU TRYING TO DO?
I'M STAYING OUT OF THIS ONE.
SHVR
...
I THINK KING IS THE PERFECT NICKNAME FOR YOU, YOUR MAJESTY.
WHAT'S SO BAD ABOUT BEING CALLED KING, ANYWAY? KINGS ARE COOL!
...!
WSH
I WATCHED THAT PREFECTURAL QUALIFIER GAME LAST YEAR...!

?!
...
OH.
YOU WANT ME TO THROW THE GAME FOR YOU?
SO.
...
WHAAAT ?!
THROW THE GAME OR GIVE IT EVERYTHING YOU'VE GOT, IT DOESN'T MATTER.
IT DOESN'T CHANGE THE FACT THAT I'M GOING TO WIN.
IT'S WE!
BUT TO ME, IT'S JUST LIKE PFFF! WHATEVER.
THIS GAME MIGHT BE IMPORTANT TO THE TWO OF YOU...
TOSS
TOSS
?
WIN OR LOSE, I HONESTLY DON'T CARE. BUT YOU TWO WILL BE IN TROUBLE IF YOU DON'T WIN, RIGHT?

HEY!
HEY! I WAS TALKING FIR--
HOW TALL ARE YOU?
THEY HAVE THE HEIGHT FOR IT.

WHO THE HECK ARE YOU, YOU--
YOU'RE THE OTHER FIRST YEARS WHO'RE SUPPOSED TO BE JOINING UP, RIGHT?

WHAT'RE YOU BRAGGING FOR, YAMAGUCHI?
AH! SORRY, TSUKKI.
S-S-SIX FEET!?
POINK
TSUKKI IS 6'2"!
I BET HE'LL BE 6'3" SOON.

WHAT?
WHAT'S AN ELITE LIKE YOU DOING STUCK AT KARASUNO?
YOU'RE KAGEYAMA FROM KITAGAWA DAIICHI, RIGHT?

TOMOR-ROW!!
WE'RE GONNA WIN!!

H-HEY!
YOU!!

WHOA.
THEY'RE HUGE!!
HEY! GIVE THAT BACK!
WSH
ISN'T IT PAST THE TIME FOR ELEMENTARY SCHOOL KIDS TO GO HOME TO MAMA?
GRRRR
YIKES! T-SHIRTS?! AREN'T YOU COLD?
SO ARE YOU THE TWO FIRST YEARS WHO SLAPPED THE PROBLEM CHILD LABELS ON YOUR OWN FOREHEADS YOUR FIRST DAY?

HOW? THE KID'S A SMART-MOUTHED LITTLE BRAT, THROUGH AND THROUGH.
HUH ?!
IS IT ME, OR DOES HE SEEM A LITTLE MEEKER AROUND THE EDGES THAN HE DID IN MIDDLE SCHOOL?
...
TRUE. THERE IS KAGEYAMA.
DON'T WORRY, SUGA-SAN! I'M ON THEIR TEAM!
BAFF
RIGHT. ASKING YOU WAS A MISTAKE.
...
LIKE HE KNEW HE WAS UNMATCHED ON THAT COURT...
EITHER WAY, HE'S STILL A STUCK-UP, SMART-MOUTHED, SNOT-NOSED KID.
...HE HAD THIS, I DUNNO... AIR OF ABSOLUTE CONFIDENCE ABOUT HIM...
WHEN WE WATCHED HIS MIDDLE SCHOOL GAME LAST YEAR...
FWIF
WOW. YOU REALLY ARE PRACTICING OUTSIDE.
HN?
PAFF
?!
LOOM
TOSS
THERE!
NEXT ONE FROM THE BACK!
!
ALL RIGHT! HERE I--

SHEESH! WHAT'S WITH HIM? HE GETS MAD EVERY TIME HE GETS CALLED THAT.
Though he kinda seems mad all the time.
WHAT'S SO BAD ABOUT HAVING A NOTORIOUS NICKNAME LIKE THAT?
TUMP
TCH!
BOP
OOPS!
GLARE
WSH
THE DANCING. NO...
...
I COULD BE THE..."THE GALE WIND"! WELL, BOTH OF THOSE ARE "WIND," BUT...
SOMETHING COOL, LIKE ... THE LITTLE GIANT...
I WANNA HAVE A NICKNAME EVERYBODY KNOWS TOO.
MY WHAT ...?
IT'S JUST IN YOUR NATURE, I GUESS.
YOU DON'T LIKE ANYBODY WHEN YOU FIRST MEET THEM.
FEH!
IS TOMORROW GOING TO TURN OUT ALL RIGHT?
STILL, THERE'S NO DENYING THEY'RE MORE THAN WE EXPECTED.
I DON'T THINK I LIKE THOSE NEW KIDS.

GYMNASIUM 2
YOU TWO LOOK AWFULLY SLEEPY.
YAAAAAWN...
URK
NN...
IT'S NICE TO MEET YOU, UPPER-CLASSMEN!
TMP
!!
?
NOW THAT YOU'RE HERE, I'D LIKE TO INTRODUCE YOU TO THE OTHER FIRST YEARS WHO ARE JOINING UP.
AH WELL.
Y-YEAH! STUDYIN'! ALL NIGHT LONG!
I, UH, I GUESS I MUST'VE STAYED UP TOO LATE STUDYING.
O-OH, UH, REALLY?
DWUH ?!
IDIOT! EVERYBODY KNOWS YOU DON'T STUDY!!
MUTTER
STUPID KING.
HOP
HOP
GRR
IF YOU COULD RECEIVE THE BALL, THAT WOULDN'T BE A PROBLEM!
HEY!!
ME?! I TOLD YOU TO GO EASY WHEN WE'RE OUTSIDE!
NOW LOOK WHERE YOU SENT IT!!

THINKING ABOUT IT...
IT'S AT LEAST BETTER TO PLAY THEM THAN TO FACE OFF AGAINST A TEAM OF UPPER-CLASSMEN, RIGHT?
I WONDER WHAT THE OTHER FIRST YEARS WE'LL BE PLAYING ARE LIKE.
I GET THAT YOU GET IT! NOW CONCEN-TRATE!!
OH YEAH. THEN THERE'S THAT THING ABOUT YOUR NEEDING TO WIN TO PLAY SETTER OR SOMETHING, RIGHT?
AAARGH! HE PISSES ME OFF!
HE PISSES ME OFF SO BAD!! BUT...
HEY! I WAS JUST ABOUT TO SAY THAT!
GRR
POINT
DON'T DO THAT!
HEY!
TCH !!
IT DOESN'T MATTER WHO WE'RE PLAYING.
WE DON'T HAVE ANY CHOICE BUT TO WIN.
BRING IT!!
FWISH
I'LL BUST THROUGH ANY WALL THE OTHER TEAM THROWS AT ME.
THIS TIME ...
A REAL SETTER WHO WILL SET THE BALL FOR ME!
NOW I HAVE A REAL SETTER ON MY TEAM!

HUP, TWO!
HUP, TWO!
MOVE YOUR FEET FIRST!
DON'T MOVE JUST YOUR HANDS!
SINCE I MADE "THE KING" DO SOMETHING, DOES THAT MEAN I OUTRANK HIM NOW? AM I NOBILITY NOW?
...
WHAT OUTRANKS A KING?
Of course we're gonna-- Ulp! Bleeaaargh...
I DON'T REMEMBER THE PART WHERE I THREW UP TOO WELL...
BUT I KNOW FOR A FACT THAT I! MADE THE KAGEYAMA! SET THE BALL! FOR ME!!
HEH HEH HEH HEH HEH HEH HEH HEH HEH HEH HEH HEH HEH HEH HEH HEH
THEN THEY'LL LET US IN THE GYM!
TOMOR-ROW WE'RE GONNA WIN!
AND WE CAN FINALLY START PRACTICING FOR REAL!
OOH! MAYBE A GOD--
!!
ZIP
OW!
QUIT DAYDREAMING AND CONCENTRATE!! THE 3-ON-3 IS TOMORROW!!
BURFF?!
I KNOW THAT!

CHAPTER 5:
The King of the Court

CHAPTER 5

"THE VOLLEYBALL PLAYER IS NOT A SOLOIST BUT A MEMBER OF AN ORCHESTRA... WHEN THE PLAYER BEGINS TO THINK, 'I AM SPECIAL,' THAT PLAYER IS FINISHED."

--COACH BERNARDO REZENDE, COACH OF THE BRAZILIAN MEN'S VOLLEYBALL TEAM, THE #1 RANKED VOLLEYBALL TEAM IN THE WORLD

FROM THE BOOK THE MAN AND THE SYSTEM THAT MADE BRAZILIAN VOLLEYBALL THE BEST, *BY NORIKO YONEMUSHI.*

PUBLISHED BY TOHO PUBLISHING CO., LTD.

RYUNOSUKE TANAKA

KARASUNO HIGH SCHOOL
CLASS 2-1

POSITION: WING SPIKER

HEIGHT: 5'10"
WEIGHT: 151 LBS.
(AS OF APRIL, 2ND YEAR IN HIGH SCHOOL)

BIRTHDAY: MARCH 3

FAVORITE FOOD:
MELON-SHAPED BREAD

CURRENT WORRY:
HE WENT TO HELP A FIRST-YEAR GIRL WHO LOOKED LOST, AND SHE STARTED CRYING.

ABILITY PARAMETERS
(5-POINT SCALE)

IF WE USED TO BE THE GREATEST ENEMIES, THEN NOW...
?!
"IF KAGEYAMA USED TO BE YOUR GREATEST ENEMY..."
WE'RE THE GREATEST TEAMMATES.
WATER!!
OF COURSE WE'RE GONNA--
OF CO ...
ULP! BLEEA ...
AARGH ...
HUFF
AH ...
HUFF
HARUMPH

"I BUGGED MY FRIEND ON THE BASKETBALL TEAM TO THROW THE BALL FOR ME."
...
HE SET IT!!
HE CAN STILL JUMP!
WOW!
YEOWCH!
"NO MATTER HOW GREAT WE GOT ALONG...I COULDN'T EVER REALLY BE TEAMMATES WITH THEM."
HE LOOKED REALLY FREAKIN' HAPPY ABOUT IT TOO.
NOT ONLY THAT...
THE SQUIRT ACTUALLY MANAGED TO HIT THAT THING.

?
TO US, IT'S TOTALLY NORMAL FOR THERE TO BE A REGULAR SETTER...
...WHO'LL PUT THE BALL UP FOR US ANYTIME WE WANT.

WE'RE GOING TO WIN.

HRP ...!
HUFF HUFF
YO.

?
THIS SATURDAY ...

KOFF!
GAK!
ULP!
WHEEZE
WHEEZE
TMP
BUT I THINK, TO HINATA... IT'S SOMETHING SPECIAL.

BAM

BUT...
TOTTER
TOTTER
I DON'T THINK HE'S GOT THE ENERGY LEFT TO SPIKE--
WHEEZE
HUFF
PUFF
!
STAGGER
...!!
FWIF
HE SET THE BALL FOR HINATA?!
?!
A SET?!
HE SMILED ?!
TMP
TMP

...
WIFFLE
HINATA, THAT WAS AWE-SOME!!
"I DON'T THINK YOU'RE NECESSARY TO WIN AT ALL."
"I'LL SET IT FOR ANYBODY WHO I THINK IS GOING TO SCORE POINTS."
HUH?
TUP
"I DON'T WANT TO LOSE ANYMORE."
"SEE, UM...
SWEEP
"WE HAVEN'T LOST YET, RIGHT?"

...TO TAKE ONE MORE STEP FORWARD.
BAMP
HOO!
HOLY COW, IT'S UP!
!!
SPLAT
GAK!
烏野高校

!!
WHY, THAT LITTLE ...!
WHEEZE
THE BALL ...!! HASN'T ...!!
GRAWR
BA SH
!
HUFF HUFF
TOUCHED THE GROUND YET ...!!
PUFF
PUFF
AH
GEEZ, KAGEYAMA! YOU JERK!
OOPS!
I GOT TICKED OFF AND HIT IT TOO FAR.
Who could get that one?!

ASIDE FROM HEIGHT AND STRENGTH...
...AND FROM HIS ATHLETIC TALENT...
BUT JUST AS MUCH A WEAPON.
...
EVEN BACK IN MIDDLE SCHOOL ...
...HINATA'S ATHLETICISM WAS IMPRESSIVE.
...SOMETHING JUST AS IMPRESSIVE--HIS DRIVE TO WIN.
HNGH
IT'S THAT RARE ABILITY...
EVEN AFTER YOU'RE DEAD TIRED. EVEN WHEN EVERYTHING HURTS...
...HE HAS SOME-THING ELSE...
ASIDE FROM THAT, I THINK...
BUT...

DUN
BUH?

UHH... HOW LONG HAVE THEY BEEN AT THIS?
FOR THE 15 MINUTES SINCE I GOT HERE, AT LEAST.
STRAIGHT?
YEAH.
GEH!
ULG!

BASH
BAFF
BISH
BOFF

BAFF
YOU'VE GOTTA BE HITTING YOUR LIMIT BY NOW!

IT'S TIME TO CALL IT--
NOT YET!!

SHEER, PURE ATHLETICISM. ENOUGH TO COVER FOR HIS POOR SKILLS AND THEN SOME.
BUT...

BAMP
!
5:30 A.M.
SNAP
HEY!
DON'T GO EASY ON ME!
...HE WASN'T ABLE TO RECEIVE BALLS THAT FAST.
FWIF
JUST A FEW DAYS AGO...
SHOOP
AND WHOOPS! RUN RIGHT INTO A PRETTY GIRL WITH TOAST IN HER MOUTH!
HEH HEH.
TMP TMP TMP TMP
...
TMP TMP
BAM
TURN ROUND THE CORNER ...
TMP TMP TMP BAM
SHUNTER
SHUNTER
I'M LATE, I'M LATE!
CRUD, I OVER-SLEPT. OH NOES!
YOU ASKED FOR IT!!
BAM
BA
MP

DOESN'T THAT MEAN HE'S YOUR GREATEST TEAMMATE NOW?
...
...
WEEEELLLLLL...
SKWEEEEEZ
...
"I DON'T THINK YOU'RE NECESSARY TO WIN AT ALL."
THURSDAY...
TATAM
TMP
TMP
TAM
TMP
FRONT!!
TUESDAY. 4:50 P.M.
HIYAAAHH!!
WEDNESDAY. 6:20 A.M.
YEAH!!
ANYWAY! LET'S PRACTICE YOUR RECEIVING, SHALL WE?
TUESDAY 12:40 P.M. ...
12:30 P.M.
MILK
WEDNESDAY...

WHAT I WANT IS TO GET GOOD ENOUGH TO BEAT KAGEYAMA.
IF I'M THAT GOOD, I'M SURE I'LL BE ABLE TO HOLD MY OWN AGAINST OTHER REALLY GOOD PLAYERS...
...AND I WON'T LOSE GAMES THAT EASILY.
UHHH ...
?
IS HE PRACTICING EVEN DURING LUNCH?
SEE, UM...
I DON'T WANT TO LOSE ANYMORE.
...
IF KAGEYAMA USED TO BE YOUR GREATEST ENEMY...
?
UGH. Y-Y... SSSS ...
YEEEH ...
UM! Y-Y-Y ...
HE REALLY DOESN'T WANT TO SAY YES, DOES HE.
...
HUNH.
TMPTMP
...IN YOUR MIND, RIGHT NOW KAGEYAMA IS THE BEST OF ANYBODY YOUR AGE. RIGHT?
SO IN OTHER WORDS ...
OKAY.
GEH!

AFTER THAT...
RRRMMMMMM
I HATED IT WHEN HE STOOD ACROSS THE NET FROM ME.
I CAN UNDERSTAND THAT, YEAH.
I think it traumatized me.
WHEN I PLAYED KAGEYAMA IN THAT GAME, HE WAS TALL AND FAST AND DID EVERYTHING RIGHT...
HE WAS JUST REALLY, REALLY GOOD.
MOO-MOO MILK
MOO-MOO MILK
YOGHURT
YOGHURT
yaaawn
BIP
AHH.
OKAY.
...I CAME TO KARASUNO THINKING THAT I WOULD SOMEDAY CHALLENGE HIM IN A GAME AND BEAT HIM.
HUH?
YOU PLAY VOLLEYBALL BECAUSE YOU WANT TO BEAT KAGEYAMA?
?
GAP KLUNK
SO THEN, HINATA...

...
SO, UM...
I COULDN'T EVER REALLY BE TEAMMATES WITH THEM.
...OR HOW GOOD OF FRIENDS WE WERE ...
BUT NO MATTER HOW GREAT WE GOT ALONG...
GLOOOOM
...WHAT KIND OF SETTER I'D HAVE ...
"SCRUB."
...TO FIND OUT ...
"YOU SUCK."
WHEN I FINALLY CAME HERE TO HIGH SCHOOL, I WAS SUPER EXCITED...
ANY REASON YOU'RE SO DEAD SET ON COMPETING WITH KAGEYAMA?
ME, I'D TRY MY BEST NOT TO BUTT HEADS WITH THE REALLY SKILLED PLAYERS...
...KINDA FEEL LIKE I... I LOST SOMEHOW ...
...I DUNNO ...
...
THANKS, BUT, UH... IF I ASKED YOU TO SET FOR ME, SUGAWARA-SAN, IT WOULD...
I'LL PUT SOME UP FOR YOU.
HE'S NOT THE ONLY ONE. I JUST SAID I'M A SETTER TOO, Y'KNOW.
!
...
?!

FWIF
HEY, HINATA?
SNOOOOR
SNOOOOR
WHAT'S OUR FIRST CLASS AFTER LUNCH?
MATH.
LET'S HIT THE VENDING MACHINES.
DARN IT ALL!!
DING DONG DING DONG
REALLY ?!
Y-YOU WILL?!
I MEAN, PLEASE!
YOU WANT TO PRACTICE SPIKING, RIGHT?
BELIEVE IT OR NOT, I AM KARASUNO'S STARTING SETTER.
!!
?!
WANT ME TO SET THE BALL FOR YOU A FEW TIMES TOMORROW MORNING?
AFTER I HAD TO LEAVE THE CLUB...
...I ASKED THE GIRLS' TEAM SETTER OR THE HOUSEWIVES' CLUB LADIES TO SET FOR ME.
I BUGGED MY FRIEND ON THE BASKETBALL TEAM TO THROW THE BALL FOR ME.
BAP
GAH! SORRY! IT WENT IN A WEIRD DIRECTION AGAIN!
BUT ...
IN MIDDLE SCHOOL, NEVER MIND A SETTER, I DIDN'T EVEN HAVE ANY TEAMMATES UNTIL MY THIRD YEAR.
?
YEAH! I LOVE IT! IT FEELS AWESOME WHEN YOU SMASH ONE FOR A KILL, AND MOST OF ALL, IT LOOKS SUPER-COOL!!

IF I GET MY RECEIVING SKILLS UP TO PAR...
IF...
...THEN WILL YOU SET THE BALL FOR ME?
I'LL SET IT FOR ANYBODY WHO I THINK IS GOING TO SCORE POINTS.
DURING THE GAME, I MIGHT HAVE NO CHOICE BUT TO SET IT FOR YOU A TIME OR TWO.
BUT ...
THE WAY YOU ARE NOW...
I DON'T THINK YOU'RE NECESSARY TO WIN AT ALL.
...!
BESIDES, RECEIVING SKILLS AREN'T SOMETHING YOU CAN GET GOOD AT OVERNIGHT.
WHAT. A. JERK!
I DON'T SEE WHAT'S WRONG WITH LETTING HIM SPIKE A TIME OR TWO.
SKWEEEZ
WE'RE ALMOST OUT OF TIME. START CLEANING UP.
RRGH...
TOSS-TOSS
THNK
THNK
DARN ...!!

HINATA! EYES FRONT!
BOP
...!
YEAH!! I'M IN THE GROOVE, MAN!
...
C'MON! LEMME SPIKE ONE!
I WANNA SPIKE IT TOO!
...
C'MON. PLEASE ?
JUST ONCE! JUST ONE TIME FOR NOW!
...
SO WHY DON'T YOU PUT ONE UP FOR ME? PLEASE?
YOU LIKE BEING SETTER, RIGHT? YOU LIKE SETTING, RIGHT?
...
BAM
HNN!
GRAAAH!!
DURING SATURDAY'S 3-ON-3, I'M GOING TO SET THE BALL FOR TANAKA-SAN AS MUCH AS I CAN.
!
YOU CONCENTRATE ON STAYING OUT OF THE WAY AND NOT SCREWING US OVER.
LET HIM HANDLE THE OFFENSIVE SIDE OF THINGS.
?!
HE'S RIGHT!
WHY NOT?! YOU SCROOGE !
SINCE YOU CAN'T EVEN DO THAT RIGHT, YOU HAVE NO RIGHT TO DEMAND A CHANCE TO SPIKE.
A SET AND AN ATTACK ONLY HAPPEN AFTER YOU'VE RECEIVED THE BALL PROPERLY.
...
DON'T WANNA.

YO.
PEEK
?!
SUGA-SAN!
A THIRD YEAR!
H-HOW ...?

WSH
FWIF

ASKING OBVIOUS QUESTIONS. VOLUNTEERING TO KEEP THE KEY WHEN YOU'RE USUALLY THE LAST ONE TO ARRIVE...
YOU WERE ACTING REALLY SUSPICIOUS YESTERDAY, Y'KNOW.
ER!! UM!! HUH ?!

WHEW
BESIDES, THIS KINDA FEELS LIKE WE'RE DOING SPECIAL SECRET TRAINING. IT'S EXCITING!
DON'T WORRY. I WON'T TATTLE ON YOU TO DAICHI.

DOINK
BURPH!!
SPLAT

CHAPTER 4: The Greatest Teammate

TOBIO KAGEYAMA

KARASUNO HIGH SCHOOL
CLASS 1-3

POSITION: SETTER

HEIGHT: 5'11"
WEIGHT: 146 LBS.
(AS OF APRIL, 1ST YEAR OF HIGH SCHOOL)

BIRTHDAY: DECEMBER 22

FAVORITE FOOD:
PORK CURRY WITH SLOW-COOKED EGGS

CURRENT WORRY:
HE THINKS ANIMALS DON'T LIKE HIM.

ABILITY PARAMETERS
(5-POINT SCALE)

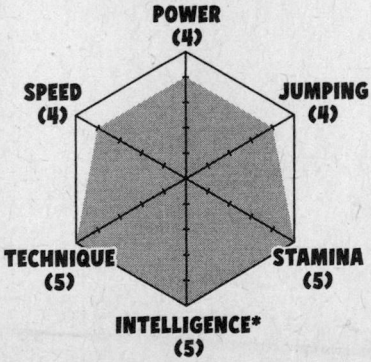

*NOTE: THE INTELLIGENCE PARAMETER ON THIS SCALE REFERS SOLELY TO INTELLIGENCE IN REGARDS TO THE GAME OF VOLLEYBALL. IT HAS NO BEARING ON NORMAL ACADEMIC PERFORMANCE WHATSOEVER.

...KARASUNO'S STRENGTH AS A TEAM WILL SKYROCKET.
DON'T YOU AGREE?
TANAKA-SAN ALREADY WENT IN, SO YOU CAN'T BE FIRST!
HECK NO! I GET TO BE THE FIRST ONE IN!
KATL KATL
SHUU
IF YOU REALLY THINK THAT, MOVE!!
SNAP
LOOKS LIKE WE'VE GOT BIGGER PROBLEMS THAN JUST PUTTING TOGETHER A COMBO WITH THOSE TWO.
OOF!
SHUU
GUYS! WE DON'T HAVE TIME--
...AND USE THEM IN TANDEM...

...ALONG WITH THOSE INCREDIBLE JUMPS.
HINATA HAS RARE NATURAL SPEED AND REFLEXES...
IN MIDDLE SCHOOL, HE WASN'T LUCKY ENOUGH TO BE ON A TEAM WITH A REAL SETTER WHO COULD SET THE BALL FOR HIM PROPERLY.
...HE HAS HINATA.
...WHO WAS DESPERATE FOR A FAST HITTER WHO COULD KEEP UP WITH HIM.
ON THE OTHER HAND, THERE'S KAGEYAMA. HE'S A HIGHLY SKILLED SETTER...
NGH!
ZIP
FASTER!
BUT IF WE CAN PUT THEIR TALENTS TOGETHER...
SEPARATE, THEY'RE INCOMPLETE.
RIGHT. HE STILL LACKS A LOT OF BASIC SKILLS.
AND YOU'RE SAYING THAT'S HINATA?! THE KID'S AN ATHLETIC FREAK, YEAH, BUT...

"Y'KNOW, DAICHI, YOU'RE BEING AWFULLY HARSH ON THOSE TWO."
Especially Kageyama.
SHOOO
VERY EXCITED
KLIK
YOU TWO REMEMBER THEIR GAME THAT WE WATCHED LAST YEAR, RIGHT?
?
DO YOU HAVE SOME SORT OF REASON FOR THAT?
...
YEAH, DAICHI-SAN. YOU'VE BEEN WAY STRICTER THAN USUAL.
BUT UNLIKE MIDDLE SCHOOL...
THERE ARE EVEN NETS!
IT'S A REAL GYM!
...ON THIS TEAM...
BUT HE LEFT NO LASTING RECORDS OR ACHIEVEMENTS.
KAGEYAMA HAD EYE-OPENING SKILL AND TALENT FOR A MIDDLE SCHOOL KID...
HE COULD RIP THE LEGS RIGHT OUT FROM UNDER THE WHOLE TEAM.
LET HIM KEEP UP THAT DIVA ATTITUDE AND HIS HIGH SCHOOL CAREER WILL GO THE SAME WAY HIS MIDDLE SCHOOL ONE DID.

TANAKA-SAN?
?!
SWSH
SWSH
IT'S STILL DARK OUT.
TMP
ARE YOU STUPID?! WE'D BE IN SO MUCH TROUBLE IF WE GOT CAUGHT!
SO LET'S FIND A WINDOW TO CRAWL IN THROUGH.
GLANCE
MAAAN, WHY DOES 5 A.M. IN THE MORNING HAVE TO BE SO STUPID EARLY?
?!
TWITCH
GRIN
WE FINISH UP BEFORE 7 A.M., GOT IT?
JINGLE
WAH HA HA! AREN'T I SUCH A GREAT UPPERCLASS-MAN?
THANKS!!
TANAKA-SAN!!
TANAKA SENPAI!!
BWAH HA HA HA! AGAIN.
TANAKA SENPAI!
SO FROM NOW ON, CALL ME "TANAKA SENPAI."
HA HA HA HA!!

T...
HUH?! UH, NO REASON! SAY, DID THE VP'S TOUPEE SURVIVE THAT HIT?
WHY?
WHA?! HEY, DON'T BRING THAT UP! PLEASE!
...
HM? YES, IT DOES.
TOMORROW AT 5 A.M....
YOU DON'T BE LATE!
DON'T BE LATE!
IT'S LOCKED.
TUESDAY
4:55 A.M.
...
...
RATL
RATL
I KINDA EXPECTED THIS, BUT...
OOPS! MY BAG! I ALMOST FORGOT IT!

TRUE.
I HAVE TO PULL MYSELF TOGETHER. HAVING THAT SECOND YEAR ON MY TEAM IS BETTER THAN JUST MY GOING IT ALONE WITH HINATA.
AND WE HAVE ALMOST A WHOLE WEEK OF PRACTICE TIME UNTIL SATURDAY.
...? WHAT'S IT MATTER IF WE WIN?
YOU ACTED REALLY CONFIDENT WE WOULD WIN EVEN AGAINST THE UPPER-CLASSMEN.
"KAGEYAMA WILL BE FORBIDDEN FROM PLAYING SETTER."
DAMN.
WHY'D IT HAVE TO BE THAT?
SUCKY ?!
OKAY! BETWEEN NOW AND SATURDAY, WE'RE GOING TO FIX YOUR SUCKY RECEIVING SKILLS!
!
ER ...
AHEM!
?
WE CAN'T USE THE GYM THOUGH.
...
HEY, SUGA-SAN! TOMORROW'S MORNING PRACTICE STARTS AT 7 A.M., LIKE ALWAYS, RIGHT?
烏野高校 排球部
HRM!!
HEM HUM HNN...
??

IT'LL BE GOING SO FAST YOU WON'T BELIEVE ANYBODY COULD ACTUALLY HIT IT...
...ZIPPING IT RIGHT PAST THE OPPOSING BLOCKERS IN THE BLINK OF AN EYE.
THEY'LL ZING THE BALL FROM ONE EDGE OF THE COURT TO THE OTHER...
...YOU CAN SEE JUST HOW AWESOME SETTERS ARE WHEN THEY MAKE SUPER-FAST SETS!
BUT THE SETTER HAS SENT IT STRAIGHT TO HIS HITTER, WHO'S ALREADY IN THE AIR.
AND THEN THAT GUY NAILS IT FOR A KILL--
BAM!
UH
OKAY. ...
IT'S THE SETTER WHO SHAKES THE OPPOSING BLOCKERS AND OPENS A CRACK IN THE WALL FOR THEM.
BEING A SETTER IS HARD AND DEMANDING AND INTERESTING AND AWESOME!
YEAH, HITTERS ARE FLASHY AND COOL.
BUT ...
BUT...
...
OKAY. I GET JUST HOW BADLY YOU REALLY WANT TO PLAY SETTER.
...

WHAT COULD BE COOLER THAN GETTING TO BE THE LEADER WHO DECIDES WHO GETS THE BALL?!
HUH ?!
BWUH?!
THE SETTER IS THE TEAM'S LEADER ON THE COURT!!
HE'S THE ONE WHO GETS TO TOUCH THE BALL MORE THAN ANYBODY ELSE!
BWAH ?!
WHAT'S WITH HIM?!
...BEING A SETTER IS HARD AND ISN'T VERY FLASHY AND STUFF...
Y-YEAH, BUT...
...IF THE SETTER WASN'T THERE TO SET THE BALL FOR YOU!
YOU WOULDN'T GET TO HIT YOUR FAVORITE SPIKES...
YEAH!
HOW ABOUT ON TV?
NO...
HAVE YOU EVER WATCHED A BIG GAME LIVE?
WSH
REALLY.
...
SITTING THERE...
WHAT YOU WANNA DO IS GO TO A LIVE GAME AND WATCH FROM THE BACK.
IT'S HARD TO SEE FROM THAT ANGLE.
OKAY. WHEN THEY SHOW VOLLEYBALL GAMES ON TV, IT'S SET UP TO GIVE YOU A SIDE VIEW OF THE COURT, RIGHT?
?

RRRRMMMMM
GRMBL GRMBL
...
...
YEAH, DAICHI-SAN. YOU'VE BEEN WAY STRICTER THAN USUAL.
Y'KNOW, DAICHI, YOU'RE BEING AWFULLY HARSH ON THOSE TWO.
...
Especially Kageyama.
DO YOU HAVE SOME SORT OF REASON FOR THAT?
HITTERS ARE WAY COOLER THAN BORING OL' SETTERS!
FREEZE
BESIDES ... SOMEONE LIKE YOU COULD BE A STARTER AT ANY POSITION.
STMP
STMP
STMP
YOU'RE GOOD ENOUGH TO BE MORE THAN A SETTER.
THE CAPTAIN HAS A POINT THOUGH.
WHAT'S WITH YOU? MAD YOU'RE THE ONLY ONE WHO GETS PUNISHED?
GYAAAH !!
YANK
YOU STUPID MIDGET SCRUB!!
BAM GOES THE WILL--
SUPPRESS
TWITCH

BATAM
7:30 P.M.

SHOOO
...
Tp
Tp

MONDAY
OOOOO
Rgh!

GOOD.
WHRL

ADDING A SKILLED THIRD PLAYER TO THEIR TEAM...
...WILL ONLY HIGHLIGHT HOW MUCH THOSE TWO AREN'T WORKING TOGETHER.
Tp
Tp

YOU SURE ABOUT THAT?
LETTING TANAKA PLAY WITH THEM, I MEAN.
HE'S GOOD ENOUGH TO BE A BIG HELP.
Tp
Tp

CONNECTING IS CRUCIAL IN VOLLEYBALL. A TEAM THAT'S DISJOINTED...
...IS WEAK.
WE'RE ALREADY SADDLED WITH A NOVICE LIKE HINATA.
A DIVA ON TOP OF THAT WOULD KILL US.
...
Tp
Tp

...!
...THE WHOLE TEAM WILL LOSE GAMES THEY COULD OTHERWISE WIN.
WITH A DIVA FOR AN ON-COURT LEADER, SOMEONE WHO TRIES TO DO IT ALL HIMSELF AND FAILS...
IT'S NOT MEANT AS A SIMPLE PUNISHMENT.
WITH YOUR TALENT, YOU COULD EASILY HANDLE ANY OTHER POSITION.
...
IT'S NOT LIKE WE'RE KICKING YOU OUT.
WELL?
THEN I GUESS YOU HAD BETTER WIN, HUH.
...
IT'S BECAUSE YOU THINK YOU CAN WIN ALONE THAT YOU TRIED THIS, RIGHT?
I'M HERE TOO!
HUH? WHAT ABOUT ME?
THE GAME WILL BE THIS SATURDAY MORNING.
I'M RIGHT HERE!
DON'T FORGET ME!
I AM!!
A SETTER!!
?!

ME? WHY ME?!
YOU SAID YOU LIKED THEIR TYPE.
BUT DEALING WITH 'EM IS A PAIN IN THE BUTT!!
...
?!
ON THE DAY OF, YOU PLAY ON THEIR TEAM.
TANAKA.
IF IT'S 3-ON-3, WHO'S GOING TO BE OUR THIRD PERSON...?
BUT ...
HUH?
A 3-ON-3 MATCH AGAINST OTHER FIRST YEARS...
IT'S A GAME WE HOLD EVERY YEAR AFTER THE NEW KIDS JOIN SO WE CAN GET A FEEL FOR HOW THEY PLAY.
AT LEAST AS LONG AS WE THIRD YEARS ARE STILL AROUND...
KAGEYAMA WILL BE FORBIDDEN FROM PLAYING SETTER.
THAT'S WITH OUR ADVISOR'S PERMISSION, OF COURSE.
AND HERE I THOUGHT YOU WERE THE ONLY ONE OF US WHO HAD WHAT IT TAKES TO KEEP PROBLEM CHILDREN IN LINE.
GOOD.
MAAAN, TWIST MY ARM, WHY DON'TCHA! GUESS I CAN DO IT! YOU HAPPY NOW, KID? BET YOU ARE!
WAP
URF!
URK
SO.
IN THE EVENT THAT YOUR TEAM LOSES...
??
HUH? THAT'S IT?
CAP-TAIN.
WHAT ...?

...
BUT IF I SHOW THAT I CAN WIN A GAME WITH HINATA ON MY TEAM, THEY SHOULDN'T HAVE ANY COMPLAINTS.
THERE'S NO OBJECTIVE WAY TO PROVE THAT WE THINK OF EACH OTHER AS TEAMMATES ...
YES! WE SAID IT IN UNISON!
THAT SHOULD SEEM TEAMMATE-LIKE.
URK!
I WILL ACCEPT WHATEVER PUNISHMENT YOU DEEM FIT.
AND IF YOU LOSE?
ACTUALLY, THIS IS PERFECT.
...
REALLY.
BESIDES THE TWO OF YOU...
...WE HAVE A FEW OTHER FIRST YEARS SLATED TO JOIN UP.
LET'S HAVE YOU PLAY THEM 3-ON-3.
!

ONE... TWO...
...
YER KIDDING! THEY REALLY DID IT!!
!!
THE TWO OF US VERSUS TWO OF YOU!
WE CHALLENGE YOU TO A GAME!
WE'LL PROVE THAT WE CAN PLAY TOGETHER ON THE SAME TEAM!!
BUT Y'KNOW? I CAN'T SAY I DON'T LIKE THAT TYPE!
...
I HEARD A "ONE, TWO"...
WHAT'D I TELL YA?! NOT A BRAIN CELL BETWEEN 'EM!!
BWAH HA!

...INDIVIDUAL TALENT CAN CARRY A TEAM TO A DEGREE.
LIKE HE MANAGED BACK THEN...
KITAGAWA DAIICHI SUFFERS HEARTBREAKING LOSS
BUT IT CAN'T TAKE THEM TO THE TOP.
...
IF KAGEYAMA DOES STILL BELIEVE THAT HE CAN WIN ENTIRELY BY HIMSELF...
AND...
...
IT'S ALMOST AS IF...
...HE HASN'T MATURED FROM HIS TIME IN MIDDLE SCHOOL.
HAVE YOU BEEN STANDING OUT THERE ALL PRACTICE?
YOU DON'T MESS IT UP.
DON'T MESS IT UP.
WHIRL
HUH?
RATTL
YOU GUYS!
CAPTAIN!!
?!
JOLT
WHA ?!
WHO ?!
BDMP BDMP
BDMP BDMP

THAT'S MY LINE, YOU STUPID SCRUB!!
...!!
NO MATTER HOW BIG A STUCK-UP, OVERCONFIDENT JERK YOU ARE...
THEN I'M WILLING TO PUT UP WITH SOME STUFF I DON'T LIKE!
...I'LL DO MY VERY BEST TO MAKE SURE I DON'T HAVE TO LOOK AT YOU AS MUCH AS POSSIBLE!!
WHY ARE YOU MAD?!
NOW LET'S COME UP WITH A PLAN!
'KAY!
THAT'S IT FOR TONIGHT!
THOUGH ALL THEY REALLY NEED TO DO IS COOL THEIR HEADS AND SHOW THAT THEY'RE SORRY.
I'D BELIEVE IT.
EVEN THEY HAVE ENOUGH BRAIN CELLS TO RUB TOGETHER TO THINK OF DOING THAT.
...IS SOMETHING I COULD TOTALLY SEE THOSE TWO SAYING.
Don'tcha think?
"WE CHALLENGE YOU! AND IF WE WIN, LET US IN!"...
I'D EXPECT KAGEYAMA WOULD TRY TO MAKE IT WORK PURELY ON HIS OWN TALENT.
SUPPOSING THEY DID DO THAT...
BUT ...

ONLY THE BEST GET TO STAY ON THE COURT.
...
YEAH.
KITAGAWA DAIICHI SUFFERS HEARTBREAKING LOSS
...FOR ABOUT A HALF HOUR. THAT'S IT.
...
AND ONE DAY I'M GONNA GET EVEN BETTER THAN YOU!
THAT'S WHY I CAME TO KARASUNO.
... AND GET GOOD AND WIN.
THIS TIME I WANTED TO TRAIN RIGHT, FOR REAL...
...
IF WE DON'T GO TOGETHER, THEY'LL JUST KICK US OUT AGAIN.
WELL? WHAT ARE YOU GONNA DO?
TUMP
IF IT MEANS I CAN PLAY VOLLEY-BALL...
...IF I DON'T GET A CHANCE TO PRACTICE ...
BUT ...
IF I'M NOT ALLOWED TO JOIN THE TEAM ...
...THEN I WON'T EVEN BE ABLE TO GET STARTED!

...IT FELT LIKE I'D BECOME THE STAR OF THE SHOW...
...AND I WAS ALL LIKE "HOAAAAA!!" ON THE INSIDE.
"HOAAA"?
I WANTED TO STAY THERE FOREVER, BUT I ONLY GOT TO BE ON THAT COURT...
THE ONLY TIME I EVER GOT TO PLAY A REAL GAME WAS THAT ONE TIME AGAINST YOU.
?
NO PLACE TO PRACTICE EITHER, SO I DID WHAT I COULD IN THE CORNER OF THE GYM AND IN THE HALLS.
BEFORE THAT, I DIDN'T HAVE ENOUGH PEOPLE TO EVEN REGISTER A FULL TEAM.
THE HALLS ?!
THAT'S WHY...
WHEN I FINALLY STEPPED INSIDE THAT HUGE GYMNASIUM...
...AND STOOD IN THE MIDDLE OF THAT BIG, WIDE COURT...

WHAAAAA?!
YEAH, RIGHT!! LIKE I'M JUST GOING TO SAY "SURE THING, SIR!" TO THAT!!
THEN WHAT ARE YOU GOING TO DO?
...TO STAY OUT OF MY WAY. GOT IT?
...AND I MEAN YOUR BEST ...
AS FOR YOU, DO YOUR BEST...
DWAAAH?! IS HE FOR REAL?! DOES HE HONESTLY FOR SERIOUS THINK THAT?!
GOOD
TOTTER
?!
?!
WE WON'T LOSE.
NOT IF I'M ON THE TEAM.
TAM TAM
TMP TMP TMP
HANG OFF THAT SILL AND PEEK IN FROM THE OUTSIDE THE WHOLE TIME?
BTAM
!
烏野
BOING
?
IN MIDDLE SCHOOL ...
...

I'M A GUARANTEED ASSET TO THE TEAM!
THAT'S REASON ENOUGH FOR THEM TO LET ME IN!
ARGH!
I DON'T HAVE TIME FOR THIS! I'M GOING TO GO MAKE THEM LET ME IN!
IT'S BECAUSE THEY WON'T THAT WE'RE STUCK OUT HERE!
TAM TAM
TAM TAM
GO! GO!
WHIRL
BEING SHUT OUT STINKS ...
THERE'S A COURT, A NET AND BALLS ALL RIGHT THERE.
GRRRRR
HOW AM I SUPPOSED TO DISPLAY SOMETHING VAGUE LIKE A SENSE OF BEING TEAMMATES?!
Don't call me that!
GLARE
WHAP
GEEZ, YOU REALLY ARE A KING--
GAAAAH!
HOLY COW!! HOW GREAT DOES THIS GUY THINK HE IS?!
?!
Other schools wouldn't take him either!
ANYWAY, WHAT'RE WE GONNA DO?
WE'RE GOING TO CHALLENGE THEM! TWO-ON-TWO.
WE WIN, AND THEY LET US IN.
?!
B-BUT US VERSUS TWO UPPER-CLASSMEN?
WHAT IF WE LOSE?!
THAT'S THE FASTEST WAY.
PLAY TOGETHER ON THE SAME SIDE, AND THAT'LL MAKE US LOOK TEAMMATE-ISH. RIGHT?

HA HA HA!
WOW, YOU ACTUALLY DID SAY WHAT YOU THINK! THAT'S GOOD, THAT'S GOOD!
...
ALL THE SETTING, SPIKING, SERVING... EVERY-THING!
... THEN I'D RATHER DO IT ALL MYSELF.
I THINK THAT IF I'M STUCK ON THE SAME TEAM AS A SCRUB LIKE HIM...
YOU ACTUALLY SAID IT?!
THOSE ARE THE RULES OF THE GAME.
IN VOLLEYBALL, YOU CAN'T LET THE BALL HIT THE GROUND. YOU CAN'T CARRY IT. THE SAME PERSON CAN'T TOUCH IT TWICE IN A ROW.
BUT Y'KNOW ?
HOW DO YOU PLAN TO DO ALL OF THAT BY YOURSELF?
...
WHAT IS WRONG WITH YOU? ARE YOU STUPID?!
GRIN
SLAM!!
MP GRU
SIIIIIIGH

I KNOW!
BUT...
I PROMISE!! PLEEEEEASE ?!
MAN!
ARE YOU SURE ABOUT THIS, DAICHI? WE AREN'T EXACTLY SWIMMING IN NEW MEMBERS.
BESIDES ...
A TEAM IS SOMETHING THAT'S BUILT OVER TIME.
BONK
HEY, GET OUT OF THE WAY!
OW!
HEY! I'M
CAP-TAIN!
I'M SORRY, SIR! PLEASE
I GET TO TALK FIRST--
SHUT UP!!
...
BAM BAM!
I'M SORRY, CAPTAIN!
BUT I WILL HAVE THEM THINK ABOUT WHAT THEY DID AND UNDERSTAND WHY IT WAS WRONG.
I'M NOT GOING TO KICK THEM OFF THE TEAM...
HOW ARE WE SUPPOSED TO PRACTICE WITH THEM LIKE THAT?
TWITCH
RATL
PEEK
OH? AND WHAT DO YOU REALLY THINK?
...!
...
I PROMISE I'LL COOPERATE WITH HINATA!
PLEASE ALLOW ME TO JOIN PRACTICE!
...

WHAM
SHOO
UNTIL BOTH OF YOU DISPLAY AN UNDERSTANDING THAT YOU ARE TEAMMATES...
...YOU ARE HEREBY FORBIDDEN FROM PARTICIPATING IN ALL TEAM ACTIVITIES.
WHAAAT ?!
CHAPTER 3: Single-Celled Organisms
UWAAAA
P-P...
PLEASE! LET ME IN!
LET ME PLAY VOLLEY-BALL!!
I PROMISE I'LL BE N-N-NICE EVEN TO KAGEYAMA!
...
HOW DO YOU DISPLAY AN UNDER-STANDING OF BEING TEAM-MATES?!
WHY ?!
WHA ?!
AAAAAH!!
DON'T ASK ME!
URK!
...!!

SHOYO HINATA

KARASUNO HIGH SCHOOL
CLASS 1-1

POSITION:
WING SPIKER (TEMP)

HEIGHT: 5'4"
WEIGHT: 114 LBS.
(AS OF APRIL, 1ST YEAR
OF HIGH SCHOOL)

BIRTHDAY: JUNE 21

FAVORITE FOOD:
EGGS OVER RICE

CURRENT WORRY:
NOT BEING ABLE TO
PALM A VOLLEYBALL.

ABILITY PARAMETERS
(5-POINT SCALE)

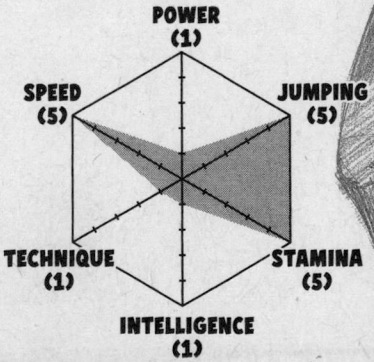

*TAG: 1-3 KAGEYAMA

I'M NOT SAYING YOU TWO HAVE TO BE EACH OTHER'S NEW BEST FRIEND.
SIDLE SIDLE
LISTEN.
URK
AND I'D RATHER NOT HAVE THE VICE PRINCIPAL GIVING US THE HAIRY EYEBALL.
烏野高

GOT IT?
?!
EEEEEEEEK

YES, IN MIDDLE SCHOOL THE TWO OF YOU MAY HAVE BEEN ON OPPOSITE SIDES OF THE NET...
...BUT HERE YOU'RE ON THE SAME SIDE. YOU NEED TO REALIZE AND ACCEPT THAT YOU'RE TEAMMATES NOW.

TOSS
TOSS

BLAP!!
CLUB SIGN-UP FORM
...ANYBODY WHO FIGHTS WITH THEIR TEAMMATES AND BRINGS DOWN THE WHOLE TEAM...
...IS NOT WELCOME HERE.

...OR HOW EARNEST AND GUNG HO AS A ROOKIE...
?

NO MATTER HOW TALENTED YOU ARE AS AN ATHLETE...
?

...WILL WE LET THEM CALL US CLIPPED-WINGED CROWS.
LOTS OF TEAMS SAY THEY'RE GOING TO NATIONALS BECAUSE THEY FIGURE THEY MIGHT AS WELL DREAM BIG.
?!
HEY!!
IDIOT! WHAT'RE YOU--
I KNOW.
DON'T WORRY.
WOO
I'M DEAD SERIOUS.
BUT TO DO THAT, ALL OF US HAVE TO COME TOGETHER AS A TEAM.
...!
YOU FOOL!
...THAT THE LITTLE GIANT DID...!
...AND STAND ON THE SAME COURT...

WE'RE GOING TO GO THERE AGAIN.
FLAP FLAP
NEVER AGAIN...
OOSH
I'M GOING TO GO...

GYMNASIUM 2
"THE FALLEN CHAMPIONS" ...
AND "THE CLIPPED-WING CROWS."
A FEW YEARS AGO...
KARASUNO'S VOLLEYBALL TEAM WAS ONE OF THE TOP IN THE PREFECTURE.
ONE TIME WE EVEN MADE IT TO NATIONALS.
NOWADAYS WE AREN'T WEAK, BUT WE AREN'T ALL THAT GREAT EITHER.
AT BEST, WE'D SQUEAK INTO THE TOP EIGHT SCHOOLS.
OTHER SCHOOLS HAVE TAKEN TO CALLING US...
MISAKA ELECTRON
!
HE'S LIKE A LITTLE GIANT!!
...
YEAH, CAN YOU BELIEVE IT? I WANNA FIND THE GUY...
...WHO CAME UP WITH THOSE DUMB NAMES AND HAVE A WORD WITH 'IM.
I STILL REMEMBER THE YEAR WHEN KARASUNO QUALIFIED FOR NATIONALS IN THE SPRING TOURNAMENT.
STUDENTS FROM THE NEARBY HIGH SCHOOL...SOME OF THE SAME KIDS I'D PASS BY ON THE STREET...
...WENT TO TOKYO TO PLAY IN A HUGE STADIUM AGAINST THE BEST OF THE BEST FOR TENS OF THOUSANDS OF FANS.
JUST THE THOUGHT IS ENOUGH TO GIVE ME SHIVERS.
KAW
FWUF

HALF AN HOUR LATER...
FLAP
SAWAMURA, COME WITH ME FOR A MOMENT.
...
...
ALL OF YOU PRETEND NONE OF THIS EVER HAPPENED. YOU SAW NOTHING.
HOW-EVER ...
WHEW
FORTUNATELY, THERE WILL BE NO OFFICIAL PUNISHMENT, AND WE AREN'T REQUIRED TO APOLOGIZE.
SCRUB!
NOW I FEEL LIKE A DOPE FOR BELIEVING YOU.
YEAH, RIGHT!
YOU'RE NOT WHO YOU WERE LAST YEAR? HAH!
YOU SUCK!
THIS IS YOUR FAULT FOR SCREWING UP SO BAD.
NOW AS FOR YOU TWO--
HEY, GUYS?
Y-YOU DON'T HAVE TO GO THAT FAR!
BUT I'M SURE YOU BOTH CAME HERE LOOKING TO WIN.
I HAVE NO IDEA WHAT MADE EITHER OF YOU CHOOSE TO ATTEND KARASUNO...
OF COURSE.
RIGHT!
...?
TWITCH
COULD I HAVE YOUR ATTENTION FOR A SEC?
LISTEN.

WOP
!
CRUD!
I'M SORR --
-- EEE?!
FWISH
!!

!!!!!!!!
?!

AHA-HEM!! YOU TWO... BFFF!...YOU TWO SHUT UP NOW...
YOU JUST NOTICED? EVERYONE FIGURED THAT OUT DURING THE ENTRANCE CEREMONY!
HUH? THAT WAS A TOUPEE?
TANA-KA, YOU SHUT UP TOO!
SNFF
...

URK!
DAICHI!

...

FWUF
!!

!
HE REACTED TO THAT QUICKLY !
GET RIGHT IN FRONT OF THE BALL AND--
GABAP
GURF !!
BLAT
ZING
BLAH BLAH

HOW IS THAT DIFFERENT FROM LAST YEAR?
WHAT THE HECK!
WHOA! I DUNNO IF I COULDA GOT THAT ONE EITHER!
NOBODY ON THE GIRLS' TEAM OR IN THE HOUSEWIVES' CLUB COULD SERVE THE BALL LIKE THAT!!
SIGH
...?
SPLAT
WHAT THE HECK WAS THAT?!
...?!
GUYS!
HRM. NOT LISTENING TO THEIR CAPTAIN'S ORDERS IS PROBLEMATIC.
DUN
ONE MORE.
BAM
TMP
TMP
TMP
ZWIP
SWF

WOOM
ACK! NOBODY SAID ANYTHING ABOUT THIS!!
FAAACE!!
SWO
GYAAA!
TOO FAST!
EEP!!
WSH
ZING
IF I CATCH IT WITH MY FACE, I'LL DIE!!
PAN

?!
HEY! YOU REALLY SHOULD KNOCK IT OFF...
TMP
TMP
TMP
WAIT ...
HE SMILED ?!
ARE THOSE TWO FIRST-YEAR STUDENTS ?
GRRR
ALL RIGHT, YOU TWO. THAT'S ENOUGH OF THAT.
GOOD.
BECAUSE I'M NOT WHO I WAS EITHER.
MATTER HOW GOOD YOU'VE GOTTEN,-- I'M NOT GOING EASY ON YOU!
SWFF
HERE I COME.
CALM DOWN. THERE'S NO REASON TO GET SCARED. I PRACTICED RECEIVING SERVES WITH THE HOUSEWIVES' CLUB A WHOLE LOT.
BATAM
BAM
TP TP
TMP
TMP
A JUMP SERVE?!
LAST YEAR HE JUST USED A REGULAR OVERHAND ONE!
?!
TMP
ZW
IP

SERVE.
ARE YOU LISTENING TO ME?!
THE VP LOVES TO LABEL STUFF PROBLEM BEHAVIOR ANY CHANCE HE GETS!
YOU TWO! EASE OFF!
RIGHT?
FIGHTING? NO, NO! OF COURSE NOT! IT'S JUST A LITTLE, ER, FRIENDLY RIVALRY!
PSST
...
YOU SERVE.
I'LL RETURN THEM. ALL OF THEM.
CUZ LAST YEAR I ONLY MANAGED TO RECIEVE ONE.
...?
HEY!!
!
YOU AREN'T WHO YOU WERE...
SWFF
?
HUH.
I'M NOT WHO I WAS LAST YEAR.
DIDN'T HE CATCH THAT ONE WITH HIS FACE?
Bla!!
Oof!
WITH MY FACE, BUT...
MY TEAMMATES, THE GIRLS' TEAM, THE HOUSEWIVES' CLUB...
I HAVEN'T BEEN DOING NOTHING. I'VE PRACTICED HARD AND GOT HELP FROM LOTS OF PEOPLE.
...

LISTEN, GUYS.
YOU DO REALIZE THAT YOU AREN'T OPPONENTS ANYMORE, RIGHT? YOU'RE TEAMMATES NOW.
VOLLEYBALL IS A GAME THAT'S ALL ABOUT CONNECTING. THE IMPORTANT THING IS WORKING TOGETHER TO--
I CHALLENGE YOU.
RIGHT NOW!
HEY!! DAICHI-SAN ISN'T DONE TALKING YET!
AT WHAT?
AT VOLLEY-BALL! DUH!!
HOW ARE WE SUPPOSED TO DO THAT ONE-ON-ONE?
HUH?!
UHHH ... LIKE WITH PASS-ING 'N' STUFF ...?
HOW CAN YOU WIN OR LOSE AT PASSING?
...!!
SHUT YER YAPS AND LISTEN !!
TMP
IT'S AWFULLY NOISY IN HERE.
PEEK
!
THIS IS THE VOLLEYBALL CLUB, RIGHT? NO ONE'S FIGHTING, RIGHT?
GAH! IT'S THE VP!
VICE PRINCI-PAL!
WSH
I MEAN, THE VICE PRINCI-PAL!

HEH. BET HE DOESN'T HAVE MANY FRIENDS.
HEY, KAGEYAMA. DID YOU REALLY HAVE TO PUT IT THAT WAY?
WHAT WAS THAT ...?
HUH?
A FIGHT ALREADY? ISN'T THAT A LITTLE QUICK?
...AND YOU'LL JUST FLUSH ANOTHER THREE YEARS DOWN THE TOILET.
KEEP MESSING AROUND LIKE BEFORE...
I DID THE BEST I--
...!
...AND ALL IT GOT ME WAS THAT UGLY LOSS.
KITAGAWA DAIICHI
YUKIGAOKA
252 08
YEAH, I DID MY BEST...
BUT...
BUT...!
...
...YOU HAVE NO RIGHT...
...TO MAKE IT SOUND LIKE EVERYTHING I DID WAS MEANINGLESS!

EVEN THOUGH I'M SHORT, I CAN FLY!
I'M GOING TO BE KARASUNO'S NEW ACE!
!
WE WATCHED YOUR MATCH AT LAST YEAR'S TOURNAMENT.
!
UM?
TH-THANK YOU, SIR!
UM!
BUT YOU GOT GUTS, AND I LIKE THAT!
YEAH! YOU WERE SHORT AND KINDA SUCKED AT A LOT OF STUFF...
ULG! Y-YEAH, I DIDN'T REALLY GET ANY TALLER...
BUT IT DOESN'T LOOK LIKE YA GREW TOO MUCH, DIDJA?
SWISH
BUT ...!
YOU'VE GOT SOME PRETTY IMPRESSIVE JUMPS TOO.
...
HOLD IT.
IF YOU'RE DECLARING YOURSELF ACE ALREADY, THAT'D BETTER MEAN YOU ACTUALLY GOT GOOD SINCE THEN.
RIGHT?
WHAT'S WRONG WITH THAT? IT'S GOOD TO HAVE GOALS.
HEY, NOW! JUST WALKED IN THE DOOR AND ALREADY YOU'RE THE ACE? YOU GOT SOME NERVE, KID!
AH!
URK!
...

?
THE PINT-SIZED NO. 1!
?!
POINT
!!
AH!!
WHOA!
IT'S YOU!!
?!
JOLT
OKAY, I SHOULD SAY HI TOO...
I'M 5'11", SIR.
HOW TALL ARE YOU?
HELLO, SIR!!
UM...
WHOA.
CHATTER CHATTER
HELLO!
HI?
HNN?
?
UM, EXCUSE ME, B-BUT HELLO!!!
WOW, NOW THIS IS A SURPRISE.
HUNH!
FWIP
HUH? UMM...
THIS IS YOU...?
THEN THE "HINATA" ON THIS OTHER SIGN-UP FORM...
?!
!
OH!
WHAT?
?
SO YOU BOTH CAME TO KARASUNO...!
烏野

C'MON, SUGA-SAN! FIRST IMPRESSIONS ARE IMPORTANT!
STEP IT UP! STEP IT UP!
YOU GOTTA STEP UP AND SHOW THIS SNOT-NOSED LITTLE FIRST-YEAR BRAT ALL THAT THIRD-YEAR DIGNITY STUFF!
RYUNOSUKE TANAKA
2ND YEAR
WING SPIKER (WS)
WOW. YOU'VE GROWN SINCE LAST YEAR.
KOUSHI SUGAWARA
3RD YEAR
VICE CAPTAIN / SETTER (S)
BUT...
IT LOOKS LIKE KAGEYAMA IS THE TALLEST BY JUST A LITTLE...
...
MAN, THEY SEEM KINDA SCA--I MEAN, REALLY STRONG.
TANAKA, QUIT MAKING FACES!
I guess they didn't see me?
THAT'S RIGHT.
I'M FINALLY HERE! AT KARASUNO!
烏野高校
排球部
MAN, HIGH SCHOOLERS ARE ALL SO BIG!
Yeah, I'm technically one too, but...

Hn!
Hn!
TWITCH
YOU'RE KAGEYAMA, RIGHT?
I GUESS THESE ARE THE UPPER-CLASSMEN?
SIR!
GOOD TO HAVE YOU!
DAICHI SAWAMURA
KARASUNO HIGH SCHOOL
3RD YEAR
VOLLEYBALL CLUB CAPTAIN / WING SPIKER (WS)
DUN

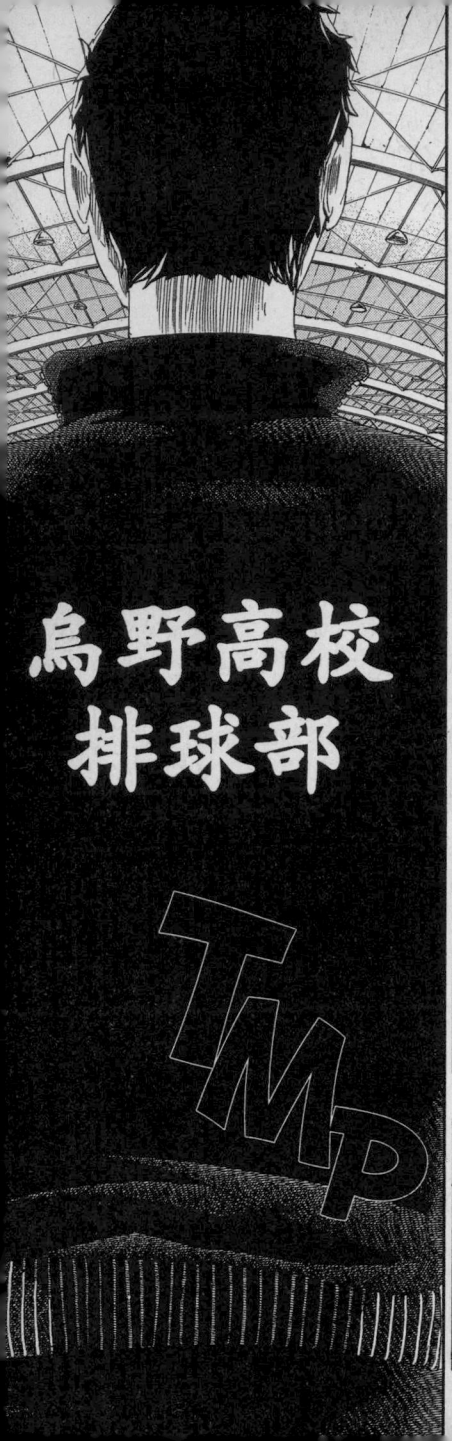

*JERSEY: KARASUNO HIGH SCHOOL VOLLEYBALL CLUB

YOU WERE RE-JECTED ?!
EVEN THOUGH YOU'RE "THE KING OF THE COURT"?!
TWITCH
YOU ...
I'M ONLY GONNA TELL YOU THIS ONCE ...
?
JOLT
?!
...
?!!
?!!!
MAN, WHO WOULDA THUNK THAT KITAGAWA DAIICHI'S STAR SETTER WOULD COME TO US, RIGHT?
GLARE
DON'T CALL ME THAT!

HOW AM I SUPPOSED TO BEAT YOU SOMEDAY IF WE'RE ON THE SAME TEAM?!
AT LEAST THAT'S THE VOW I MADE TO MYSELF WHEN I CAME TO KARASUNO, BUT WHAT ARE YOU DOING HERE?
...
AH ...!
...
HOW COME YOU DIDN'T GO TO ONE OF THOSE?!
THERE'RE OTHER SCHOOLS OUT THERE BESIDES THIS ONE THAT, Y'KNOW, SCREAM POWER-HOUSE!
I DID APPLY TO THE BEST VOLLEYBALL SCHOOL IN THE PREFECTURE...
?
...AND I WAS REJECTED.
?!

W-WHAT?
WHY'D YOU GO QUIET?
A-ARE YOU ...
...T-TRYIN' TO START SOME-THIN'?
HIS RIDICULOUS SPEED, REFLEXES AND JUMPING ABILITY.
TOGETHER, THEY WERE ENOUGH TO MAKE UP FOR HIS LACK OF HEIGHT AND THEN SOME.
...
WE HAVEN'T LOST YET, RIGHT?
Hinata
Hinata
!
YOU'RE THAT STUPID SHORT KID WHO SUCKED!!
HE DIDN'T HAVE THE FIRST CLUE HOW TO USE IT!
GLARE
BUT, DESPITE HAVING ALL THAT ...
?!
BUT...
NEXT TIME, I'M GONNA WIN!!
YEAH, YOU THRASHED US IN THAT ONE GAME...
H-HEY.
DON'T THINK YOU CAN MAKE FUN OF ME ANYMORE.

TOBIO KAGE-YAMA!
WAIT... MAYBE I HAVE THE WRONG GUY...?
WHAT'S HE DOING AT KARASUNO ?!
NO...
NUH-UH.
"WHAT THE HECK HAVE YOU BEEN DOING THE LAST THREE YEARS?!"
"WHY ARE YOU EVEN HERE?"
"THAT'S WHY YOU GET MADE FUN OF."
NO DOUBT ABOUT IT. THIS IS--
I'LL NEVER FORGET THAT SMUG FACE OR ALL THOSE NASTY THINGS HE SAID TO ME.
GRRR
I DON'T KNOW YOUR NAME.
...
I SAW YOU LAST YEAR. YOU'RE... UHH...
YOU...
NO. I REMEMBER YOU.
?!
...
I BET YOU DON'T REMEMBER THE TEAM THAT YOU WHOPPED IN THE FIRST ROUND, BUT I--
M-MY NAME IS SHOYO HINATA, AND D-DON'T YOU F-FORGET IT!!

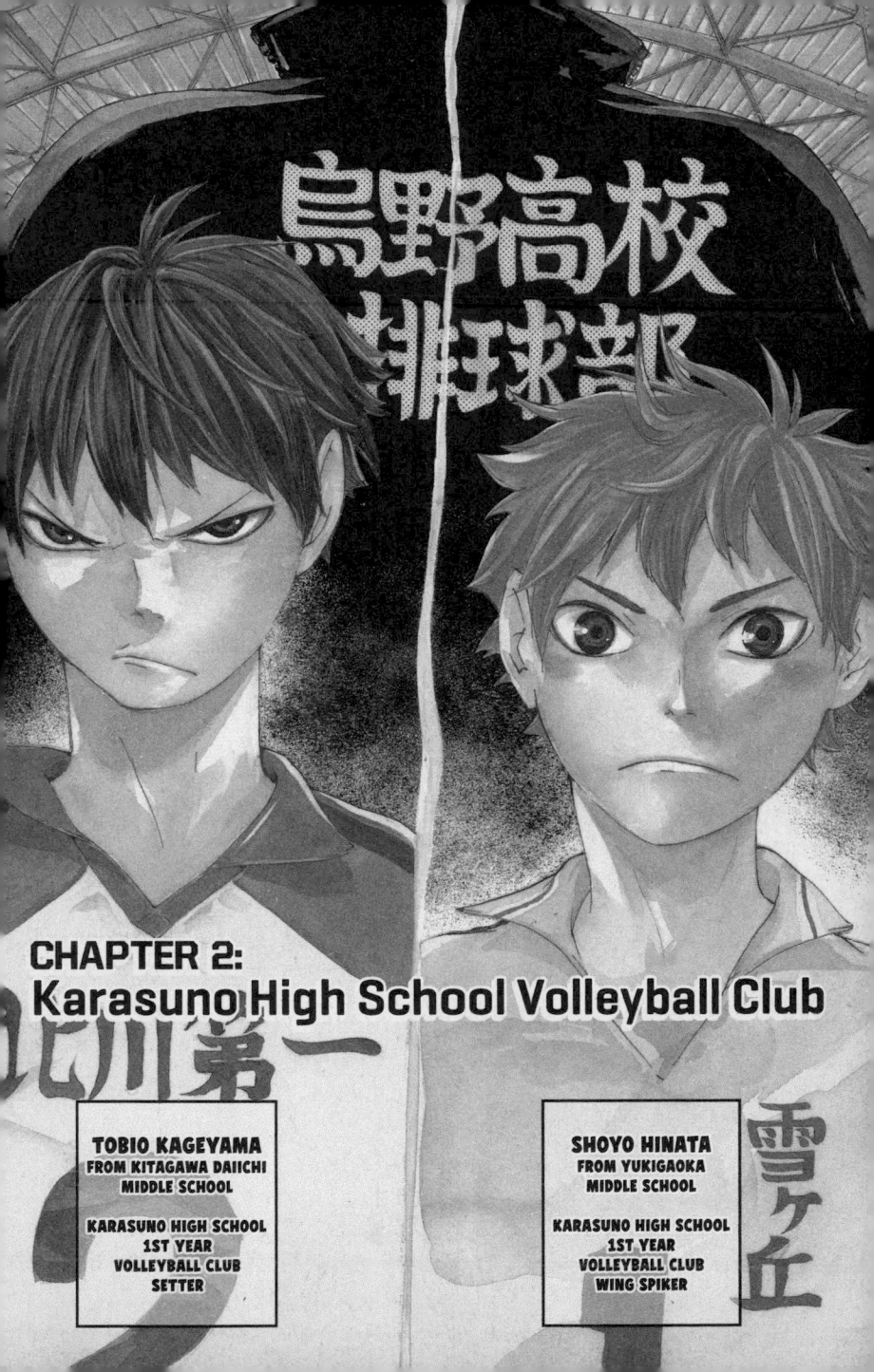

CHAPTER 2:
Karasuno High School Volleyball Club

TOBIO KAGEYAMA
FROM KITAGAWA DAIICHI MIDDLE SCHOOL

KARASUNO HIGH SCHOOL
1ST YEAR
VOLLEYBALL CLUB
SETTER

SHOYO HINATA
FROM YUKIGAOKA MIDDLE SCHOOL

KARASUNO HIGH SCHOOL
1ST YEAR
VOLLEYBALL CLUB
WING SPIKER

CHAPTER 2
DURING MIDDLE SCHOOL...
...IN MY ONE AND ONLY OFFICIAL TOURNAMENT...
...MY TEAM LOST IN THE FIRST ROUND. WE WERE CRUSHED.
OUR OPPONENT WAS "THE KING OF THE COURT."
I WAS SURE HE WAS GOING TO GO ON TO ONE OF THE TOP HIGH SCHOOLS IN THE PREFECTURE...
...AND I WAS GOING TO BEAT HIM AND GET MY REVENGE. I SWORE THAT TO MYSELF...
...WHEN I CAME HERE, TO KARASUNO HIGH.
BUT--
WHA...
WHAT ARE YOU DOING HERE?!
?!

BUT MAYBE... JUST MAYBE... IF I **WASN'T** ALONE...

WHAT ARE YOU DOING HERE?!

?!

*JERSEY: KARASUNO, 1-3 KAGEYAMA
TAM TAM
烏野
1-3 影山
A WALL LOOMS IN FRONT OF ME.
A TALL, TALL WALL...
WHAT'S THE VIEW LIKE OVER THAT WALL?
BATAM
WHA--
WHAT WILL I SEE BEYOND IT?
TAM
IT'S SOMETHING I COULD NEVER...
...EVER...
...SEE ON MY OWN.

HE DODGED ME?!
DONG
DMP
DMP
DMP
YEP! VOLLEY-BALL!
...JOIN ?!
ZOOM
HINATA
SATA
HERE, I CAN GET ALL THE PRACTICE I WANT!
AND THEN...
DMP
DMP
DMP
DMP
DMP
I'M AT KARASUNO HIGH SCHOOL!
I'M FINALLY HERE!
I'M HERE!
GYMNASIUM 2
AT LEAST...
BUT...
...THAT'S WHAT I THOUGHT.
...I CAN GO AND GET MY REVENGE ON HIM--THE KING!
I BET HE GOT TO GO TO ONE OF THE BEST VOLLEYBALL SCHOOLS IN THE PREFECTURE.

KIYOKO-SAN, YOU LOOK GORGEOUS AS ALWAYS TODAY!
DON'T WORRY, DAICHI! I'M SURE WE'LL GET MORE.
ONLY THIS MANY? THERE USED TO BE LOTS MORE IN THE PAST.
Thanks.
RYUNOSUKE TANAKA
KARASUNO HIGH SCHOOL 2ND YEAR VOLLEYBALL CLUB MEMBER
DAICHI SAWAMURA
KARASUNO HIGH SCHOOL 3RD YEAR VOLLEYBALL CLUB CAPTAIN
KOUSHI SUGAWARA
KARASUNO HIGH SCHOOL 3RD YEAR VOLLEYBALL CLUB VICE CAPTAIN
...
I LOVE IT WHEN YOU TOTALLY IGNORE ME TOO!
HERE.
THESE ARE THE NEW SIGN-UPS WE'VE RECEIVED.
CLUB SIGN-UP
KIYOKO SHIMIZU
KARASUNO HIGH SCHOOL
3RD YEAR
VOLLEYBALL CLUB MANAGER
IS THIS WHO I THINK IT IS?!
WHAT THE HECK?
HMM...
HN?
FLIP
CLUB SIGN-UP FORM
TO THE VOLLEYBALL
LOOM
YOU THERE! THE ENERGETIC ONE IN THE TRACKSUIT!
HAVE YOU PICKED A CLUB TO...
DMP
HNN?!
JOIN US!
WANT TO JOIN THE SOCCER CLUB?
HOW WOULD YOU LIKE TO BE THE BASEBALL CLUB'S NEW MANAGER?
JOINING THE MARCHING BAND WILL REALLY IMPROVE YOUR ABS!

HE'S LIKE A LITTLE GIANT!!
I DECIDED THAT LONG AGO!
BY BIKE...
WHRRR
...IT'S A HALF-HOUR RIDE OVER THE MOUNTAIN.
MIYAGI PREFECTURE'S KARASUNO PUBLIC HIGH SCHOOL!!
DING DONG DING DONG
SKREE
IT'S THE SPRING ...
...OF MY FIRST YEAR OF HIGH SCHOOL.
3-1
3-1
SAWA-MURA.

IT DOESN'T MATTER WHO--THE GIRLS' VOLLEYBALL TEAM...
...THE LOCAL HOUSEWIVES' INTRAMURAL TEAM...
IF THEY'LL LET ME IN, I'LL JOIN THEM.
Quit it! You're embarrassing me!
Thanks for everything today!
Again?!
BOW
TRAINING.
EXPERIENCE.
A COACH.
SOMEONE TO PRACTICE WITH.
I CAN'T WIN BY MYSELF.
I CAN'T DO THIS ALONE.
Eww! Gross, man!
My notes!
Hot Pack
I NEED TO GET INTO THE RIGHT HIGH SCHOOL SO I CAN WIN!
AND I HAVE TO STUDY FOR ENTRANCE EXAMS TOO!
THE HIGH SCHOOL I MOST WANT TO GET INTO...
Dude. Cry and get it out of your system.
No, I am not going to cry!
Ooh, gonna cry?
GRADUATION
KOUSEN MIDDLE SCHOOL ACADEMY ADVANCES TO NATIONALS
KITAGAWA DAIICHI SUFFERS HEARTBREAKING LOSS
ALONE ISN'T GOOD ENOUGH.

ONLY THE BEST.
ONLY THE WINNERS GET TO STAY ON THE COURT.
...
IF YOU WANT TO WIN...
...THEN GET STRONGER! GET BETTER!
...THAT I LACK.
THERE ARE LOTS OF THINGS...
WHRL

THEN SOMEDAY I'M GONNA BEAT YOU!!
AND I'M GONNA BE THE ONE...
...WHO GETS TO STAY ON THE COURT LONGER THAN ANYBODY ELSE!!

?
?!
SHO-CHAN ?!
DASH
TMP
?!
YOU!!
IF YOU REALLY ARE THE KING WHO RULES THE COURT...

WE HAD BAD LUCK, THAT'S ALL.
I MEAN... THE TEAM WE PLAYED IS A FAVORITE TO MAKE NATIONALS.
AH WELL. WE DID WHAT WE COULD.
...
AH.
...
TROMP
TROMP
TROMP
...WE STILL HAVE ONLY TWO OPTIONS--TO WIN OR TO LOSE.
AND IF WE LOSE ...
...WE CAN'T STAY OUT THERE ON THE COURT ANYMORE.
THAT DOESN'T MATTER.
?
EVEN IF THE OTHER TEAM IS REALLY GOOD...
...OR REALLY BAD...

KITAGAWA DAIICHI
YUKIGAOKA
ZERO.
2 5 2 0 8
SETS WON...
Ta-daaaa
CLUB SIGN-UP FORM
YEAR:
CLASS
NAME:
VOLLEYBAL
NO WAY! I'VE NEVER DONE ANY OF THAT BEFORE!
TOTAL TIME SPENT ON THE COURT...
A MERE...
...31 MINUTES.
"THE KING OF THE COURT."
TOBIO KAGEYAMA.
AFTERWARDS, I FINALLY LEARNED HIS NAME.

YOU! WHAT THE HECK HAVE YOU BEEN DOING THE LAST THREE YEARS?!
!!
DON'T, MAN.
WHAT DID YOU JUST SAY?!
...AND ONLY OFFICIAL GAME IN MIDDLE SCHOOL.
IT WAS MY FIRST...!

DOES HE HAVE THE REFLEXES...
...TO REACT TO THAT KIND OF SET?
DESPITE THAT...
...HE STILL HIT IT.
THAT ONE SPIKE WAS JUST A FLUKE.
RIGHT. THAT WAS COMPLETELY ON THE SETTER FOR SCREWING UP.
THERE'S NO WAY THEY PLANNED A QUICK SET!
GREAT ATHLETICISM.
QUICK REFLEXES.
EXCELLENT CONTROL OF HIS BODY.
AND AN UNFLAGGING DRIVE TO WIN.
IF HE HAS ALL THAT...
SHO-CHAN.
WE SHOULD LINE UP.
...
?
...
TMP

GAME OVER
FWE FWE EEE!!
FWIP
KITAGAWA DAIICHI
25
2
SET SCORES: 2-0 [25-5 / 25-8]
WINNER: KITAGAWA DAIICHI MIDDLE SCHOOL

...
THEY SURE DON'T LOOK LIKE A TEAM THAT JUST CRUSHED ITS OPPONENT IN BACK-TO-BACK SETS.
CHECK OUT THE KITAGAWA KIDS.
...

YEAH, BUT LOOK.
AAAGH!! THAT LAST ONE WAS SO CLOSE!!

THAT JUMP...
...FROM THAT AWKWARD POSITION!...
...OFF HIS BACK FOOT, NO LESS!

I COULD ONLY JUST FOLLOW HIM WITH MY EYES.

THUMP
KRAAASH
GAH! SHO-CHAN!!
SWFF
AH.
THAT WAS ONE CRAZY MATCH.
I'M...KINDA SHOCKED.
SHORTY REALLY HIT THAT!!
OH WOW!
HOO!!
FLMP
SHO-CHAN, ARE YOU OKAY?!
...LANDED OUT OF BOUNDS.
MY SPIKE...

WHOOSH
WHY IS HE SUDDENLY ON THE RIGHT?!

HE WAS THERE ON THE LEFT.
ALL IT TOOK...
...WAS ONE...
WSH
I HAD HIM MARKED.
...SINGLE BLINK.
DRAT!
SO WHY...
北川第一

YEAH!!
FREE BALL! IZUMI-SAN!!
BMP
SHO-CHAN, HERE!
LET SERVE! GET IT BEFORE IT FALLS!!
WAP
RGH ...!
BOD
Hngh!
WELL, YUKIGAOKA? NOW WHAT WILL YOU DO?
OOPS!
AT LEAST... THERE WASN'T.
THERE ISN'T ANYONE OVER THERE!
I JUST BRUSHED IT!
OH CRAP!!
NO FAULT FOR DRIBBLING, EVEN WITH TWO TOUCHES?
BUT...
A BOTCHED SET?!

?!
北川第一
?!
CHASE IT DOWN!!!
JOLT
TP TP TP
TP
YEAH, THERE'S NO WAY I COULD GET THAT.
THOSE SCRUBS AREN'T PULLING OFF A MIRACULOUS COMEBA--
WELL, YEAH... BUT CHECK THE SCORE.
THAT LAST POINT WASN'T A MIRACLE! IT WAS TAKEN!!
24 08
ARE YOU THE COACH NOW?
YEESH. GOT MORE SAND IN YOUR SHORTS THAN USUAL TODAY?
UH... SORRY.
!
THE GAME ISN'T OVER YET! QUIT SLACKING OFF!!
HE!!
STOLE !!
A POINT! FROM US!!
BUT THEY'RE STILL ON THE BRINK.
YUKIGAOKA'S NO. 1 IS GIVING IT HIS ALL...
...
Good serve!
Good luck, Shorty!!
FWEEEEEE
HE MEANT EVERY WORD OF THAT!!
AS LONG AS YOU DON'T GIVE UP--
WELL... YEAH, THAT'S TRUE, I GUESS.
Ah ha ha...

WHY KEEP FIGHTING, EVEN WHEN I'M HOPELESSLY OUTMATCHED?
ONE REASON.
BECAUSE I HAVEN'T...
...LOST YET...!
ZIP
BA-
BAM
WHAP
TIPPED IT!
COVER!!

TWITCH
SHIVER
...!!
WE HAVEN'T LOST YET, RIGHT?
DID HE REALLY NEED A FIRST YEAR TO TELL HIM THAT?
KID'S GOT A POINT.
...
YEAH, WHY BOTHER? IF I WERE IN THEIR SHOES, I WOULD'VE THROWN IN THE TOWEL A LONG TIME AGO.
...
UHHH
LMM ...
IT'S JUST ...
I DUNNO.
WELL ...
FWEEEEEEEEEE
BECAUSE IT HASN'T...
...TOUCHED THE GROUND YET.
SHO
SHO-CHAN!
THERE'S ONLY ONE REASON TO KEEP CHASING THE BALL.
HE'S RIGHT. IT'S THAT SIMPLE.
NO MATTER HOW IMPOSSIBLE IT LOOKS...
BALL'S UP!
EVERYBODY CONCENTRATE!

ALMOST ...!!

IT'S KITAGAWA DAIICHI'S MATCH POINT!
YUKIGAOKA IS TEETERING ON THE BRINK OF DEFEAT!
2 4 2 0

DOTTK
WOW!
SPLAT

TWEEP
HE ALMOST ...
HE JUST DOESN'T GIVE UP, DOES HE...
OW! THAT HAD TO HURT.

IT, UM, IT WOULD BE REALLY BAD IF YOU GOT HURT...
AND TO BE BLUNT, WE AREN'T GOING TO WIN THIS GAME.
SO WHY ARE YOU, UM... GOING SO FAR TO...?
HUH?!

SORRY! I'LL GET THE NEXT ONE.
!
UM! C-CAPTAIN ...?
?

AARRGH!
PINK
UM...
I-I'M SORRY. THAT WAS MY FAULT.
I botched the bump.

FWEEEEE!
THE FINALS ?!
THEN HOW LONG ARE YOU TWO GOING TO WAIT TO GET SERIOUS ABOUT IT?!
!
WHAT'S THE POINT IN GETTING SO WOUND UP OVER IT?
SHEESH. THE OTHER GUYS CAN'T BLOCK FOR CRAP, Y'KNOW.
GEEZ. THERE HE GOES, DEMANDING THE IMPOSSIBLE AGAIN.
YES! ANOTHER ACE SERVE! NO ONE CAN SAVE THAT.
NOT YET!
BOM
OOPS!
BAFP
NICE SERVE!!
SWF
...
QUIT IT! THE GAME'S STILL ON!
TMP TMP TMP TMP
WOW. NO WAY ANYBODY CAN CATCH THAT.
IT STILL HASN'T TOUCHED THE GROUND...!
IT STILL HASN'T TOUCHED THE GROUND...
YEAH, NOT HAPPENING.
...
DUN
!!

...IF YUKIGAOKA HAD A PROPER SETTER.
EVEN AT THAT HEIGHT, NO. 1 COULD STILL BE WAY MORE EFFECTIVE...
YEAH.
YEAH.
YEAH, SHO-CHAN! SHAKE IT OFF!
YOU CAN DO IT AGAIN, SHOYO!
STILL, THAT LITTLE NO. 1 SURE IS FLYIN' ALL OVER THE PLACE!
MAN, IF ONLY HE WAS TALLER!
EVEN THOUGH HE SUCKS AT A LOT OF STUFF.
PAT
...HE'S OUT THERE ON THE COURT PLAYING THE GAME BY HIMSELF.
IT'S ALMOST AS IF...
HE'S DOING AN IMPRESSIVE JOB OF HOLDING TOGETHER THAT TEAM OF ROOKIES ALL BY HIMSELF.
ON THE FLIP SIDE...
EVEN THOUGH HE PERSONALLY SHOULD HAVE PLENTY OF ABILITY TO DO SO.
KAGEYAMA IS SURROUNDED BY DECENT TALENT, BUT HE'S NOT MAKING THE BEST USE OF THEM.
MOVE FASTER !!
!
TCH!
NGH!
ZIP

KITAICHI STEAMROLLED THEM IN THE FIRST SET TOO.
YIKES. THE MORE I WATCH, THE MORE I PITY THOSE POOR KIDS.
KITAGAWA DAIICHI
YUKIGAOKA
222
07
DUN
TMP
TMP
TMP
HINATA-SAN!!
SHO-CHAN!!
IT'S UP!
IT SEEMS EVEN TALLER THAN BEFORE.
THE WALL IS BACK.
I CAN'T SEE THE OTHER SIDE...
...AT ALL...
BA
BAM
AH!
STUFFED AGAIN!
GAH!
LOOM

...?!
BAM
BA
THMP!
WHEN
NAH. SORRY I BOTCHED IT! YOU GOT THE BALL UP FOR ME AND EVERYTHING. I'LL NAIL IT NEXT TIME.
TMP
NICE COVER!
FRONT! FRONT!
TA-TUM.
...
UM...
SHO-CHAN, IT'S OKAY. DON'T LET IT GET TO YOU.
!
OUCH!
THEY GOT 'IM.
STILL, THAT WAS AN IMPRESSIVE JUMP.

WHOA!
GO!!
?!
HE FLEW ?!
SO THAT WASN'T A BLUFF!
can fly!
川第一
WATCH FOR THE CROSS.
!!
WSH
SWOO
WOOSH
5

AB NOD!!
?!
HINATA, WHY ARE YOU CRYING?!
AAAAAH!! DANK YU, DANK YU, DANK YUUUU!!
YOU LOOK LIKE YOU'RE BAWLING TO ME!
STAFF ROOM
CLUB SIGN-UP FORM
YEAR I CLASS C NAME: S
1ST
VOLLEYBA
2ND
THEY SAY THEY PLAYED A LITTLE IN ELEMENTARY SCHOOL.
THEN FINALLY...
STAAAKE
?!
TWO MORE PEOPLE...!
IF I CAN BEG JUST TWO MORE PEOPLE TO HELP OUT ...!
FINALLY...!!
TMP
TMP
TMP
SHO-CHAN, DO IT!!
BAP

I'LL GET PEOPLE TOGETHER AND MAKE A FULL TEAM!
UH-HUH.
BUT NEXT TIME FOR SURE!
EVERY-BODY'S TURNED ME DOWN SO FAR...
I'M SURPRISED YOU KEEP PRACTICING, EVEN THOUGH YOU CAN'T PLAY IN ANY GAMES OR ANYTHING.
One! Two! One! Two!
TOMP TOMP
HEY!
I'LL BE ABLE TO PLAY IN REAL GAMES! SOMEDAY!
THEN...
SO, KOJI? WANNA JOIN?
HOW MANY TIMES DO I HAVE TO SAY NO?
TA-DAAAH
HERE.
FWAP
AND THERE'S THREE OF THEM?!
FIRST YEARS ...?
IN THE SPRING ...
SCHOOL
HUH?
...OF MY THIRD YEAR OF MIDDLE SCHOOL...

GYMNASIUM
OKAY, GIRLS! NEXT IS RUNNING!
TMP
TMP
OKAY!
I'M ON THE BOYS' TEAM!!
NO, MAN. THINK ABOUT IT! ALL THOSE GIRLS--
I DUNNO IF I WANNA PLAY ON A GIRLS' TEAM...
OH, I KNOW! HOW 'BOUT YOU TWO JOIN TOO?
NAH.
SHO-CHAN?! HUH? SET WHAT?!
YOU'RE ON BREAK, RIGHT? COME SET FOR ME!
IZUMIN!
NO WAY! I'VE NEVER DONE ANY OF THAT BEFORE!
TMP TMP
TAM TAM
NOW'S MY CHANCE TO USE THE COURT!
DASH
YES! THE GIRLS WENT OUT RUNNING!
GATHER ROUND!
I'LL HELP YOU WITH YOUR FREE PRACTICE AGAIN.
BUT UPPER-CLASSMEN ARE WATCHING...
I CAN'T!
I WANNA PRACTICE SPIKING, BUT I CAN'T DO THAT BY MYSELF.
Underhand toss! That's it!
THAT'S ALL YOU HAVE TO DO!
JUST TOSS IT!
KAN
KAN
KAN
HEY, SHOYO?
PLUNK
AH! YESSIR!

COME PRACTICE PASSING WITH ME!
HEY, ACCHAN! ARE YOU DONE WITH YOUR CLUB?!
I PRACTICED ANYWHERE I COULD.
EVEN THE HALLS.
MUSIC ROOM
POINK
QUIT AMBUSHING ME!
WHAT, AGAIN?!
!!
WHO'S THAT?!
!
KICK
HUF! HUF! HUF!
HEY! LOOK OUT!
DO-DOINK
THE CORNER OF THE GYM...
APH!
THE CORNER OF THE FIELD...
...IN EVERY HUNDRED FAILURES GREW TO BE MORE AND MORE FUN.
AT FIRST, THAT'S ALL IT WAS. BUT LITTLE BY LITTLE, THE ONE SUCCESS ...
DID YOU SEE THAT?!
IT WENT STRAIGHT! IT WENT STRAIGHT!
BOFF
!!
OOH!
...AND KEPT GOING OUT OF STUBBORNNESS.
I STARTED ON A WHIM...
WHA?!
DID NOT!!
WELL, YEAH, THERE IS...
HE ADMITS IT!
SO WHO'RE YOU AFTER, HUH?
MOO-MOO MILK
I'M IN THE BOYS' VOLLEYBALL CLUB!
NO!! THAT'S NOT IT!!
THERE'S A HOT THIRD-YEAR GIRL, RIGHT?
2 – C
HEY, HINATA!
WE HEARD YOU JOINED THE GIRLS' VOLLEYBALL TEAM!
FOR REAL?!
BFFT!
MY ARMS HURT, AND THE BALL DOESN'T GO WHERE I WANT IT TO ANYMORE.
HAVEN'T YOU HAD ENOUGH YET? LET'S QUIT!
STING STING
THIS REALLY IS THE LAST ONE, OKAY?!
THAT'S THE THIRD TIME YOU'VE SAID THAT!
PLEASE! JUST ONE MORE!
THANKS!

AND I COULDN'T HELP BUT THINK--MAN, IT WOULD BE COOL IF I COULD BE LIKE THAT SOMEDAY.
THE NICKNAME "THE LITTLE GIANT" REALLY STRUCK A CHORD.
...BUT I STOOD THERE ENTRANCED, WATCHING THAT SMALL ATHLETE PLAY.
I DIDN'T REALLY UNDERSTAND VOLLEYBALL OR ITS RULES BACK THEN...
TO SOMEONE LIKE ME, WHO'S ALWAYS AT THE FRONT WHEN LINING UP BY HEIGHT...
EVERYBODY LINE UP!
BA-BAAN
HUH ?!
BUT ...
...I DECIDED TO PLAY VOLLEYBALL WHEN I GOT TO MIDDLE SCHOOL.
BUT WITH THE SIGHT OF THAT SMALL ATHLETE BURNED INTO MY BRAIN...
YUSHIAOKA MIDDLE SCHOOL
I LOVED LOTS OF SPORTS, LIKE BASEBALL, BASKETBALL AND SOCCER...
SOMEBODY ELSE'LL GET THE FIELD BEFORE US!
SHO-CHAN, C'MON !
N-N-NO, THANK YOU...
UM! ?!
OR DO YOU WANT TO JOIN THE GIRLS' TEAM INSTEAD?
A WHAT, NOW?
I'M GONNA BECOME A LITTLE GIANT!
I'LL RUN THE CLUB MYSELF!
OH?
AND IT'S A BOYS' VOLLEYBALL APPRECIATION CLUB, NOT A FULL TEAM.
Not enough people.
YEP. THAT CLUB KEPT GETTING SMALLER BY THE YEAR, Y'KNOW.
REALLY ?!
STAFF ROOM
OH.
WHAT WILL YOU DO? WANT TO APPLY FOR A DIFFERENT CLUB?
I'D BE THE ONLY MEMBER?

WOOSH
KREEEEE
?!
HE'S LIKE A LITTLE GIANT!
WAAAA
PON PO- PON
PON PO- PON
PON PO-
...I SAW A SHORT, BLACK-CLAD ATHLETE PLAYING FOR A SCHOOL NAMED AFTER CROWS...
...IS WHAT I HEARD THE ANNOUNCER SHOUT OVER THE TV.
THAT...
...FLYING AROUND THE COURT, SCORING POINT AFTER POINT.
WHEN I WATCHED THE TV BROAD-CAST BACK THEN...
EVERY SPRING, THERE'S A BIG HIGH SCHOOL VOLLEYBALL TOURNAMENT.
LIVE FROM THE NATIONAL SPRING HIGH SCHOOL VOLLEYBALL TOURNAMENT!
WAAAAA

I'LL JUMP RIGHT OVER WHATEVER WALL THEY TRY TO PUT IN FRONT OF ME!
KOJI!
URK!
WHAT, ME?!
BAD
BOM
NICE SERVE!
BUT I'VE GOT STRONG LEGS!
OKAY!
IZUMIN!! YOUR TURN!!
YES! IT WENT UP!!
NOT THAT I CAN SET IT LIKE THAT OTHER GUY CAN!
Oof!
TMP
GET IT, SHO-CHAN!!
BAD
OW!
NO MATTER HOW TALL IT IS!!
TMP
TMP

*JACKET: HIGH SCHOOL VOLLEYBALL CLUB

...
UNDER-STOOD?
...IT'S MAKING THE BALL EASY FOR YOUR SPIKER TO HIT.
THE IMPORTANT PART ISN'T YOUR PERSONAL SKILL...
DON'T JUST RELY ON SPEED.
COACH
LINE UP!!
...
FWEEP
YES, COACH!
PLUNK!
LOOM
URGH! MY STOMACH ...
HEY!
THANK YOU FOR THE GAME!!
BOW
FWEEEEEE
IT'S REALLY ABOUT TO START!
FINALLY...!
OOH!
THEY'RE JUST GETTING STARTED, DAICHI-SAN! SUGA-SAN!
YEAH.
ONE OF THEM'S GOT SOME ENERGY.
BDMP BDMP

BAM
NICE SPIKE!!
TMP
TMP
TMP
OH, OKAY. SO HE'S THEIR SETTER.
?
FWIF
TMP
...
SPIKE
SET
SETTER
RECEIVE
THREE TOUCHES FROM DEFENSE TO ATTACK!
HE'S THE GUY WHO TOSSES THE BALL UP AND SETS IT UP FOR THE SPIKER. DUH!
We learned this last night!
UH, WHAT'S A SETTER?
I HAVE NO IDEA WHERE HE'S GONNA SEND IT NEXT!
NO FAIR! HE'S ACTUALLY GOOD!
YOUR TIMING IS WAY OFF!!
TUP
MAN, LOOK AT HIM! HE'S PUTTING THAT BALL WHEREVER HE WANTS!
EVEN THOUGH HE'S ONLY TOUCHING THE BALL FOR AN INSTANT...
KAGE-YAMA.
TMP
ME NEITHER.
YIKES! HE'S GOOD, BUT I DON'T THINK I WANNA BE ON HIS TEAM.
SORRY.
HOW MANY TIMES DO I HAVE TO TELL YOU?! YOU HAVE TO MOVE FASTER FOR A QUICK SET!

I'M GOING TO BE THE ONE WHO WINS AND GETS TO STAY ON THE COURT!
WHAT'RE YOU DOING PISSING OFF SCARY GUYS LIKE HIM?! I THOUGHT YOU WERE GOING TO THE BATHROOM!
??
AH! IZUMIN!
?!
SHO-CHAN!
STMP
STMP
C'MON. WE'RE GOING BACK.
WHAT ABOUT YOUR QUEASY GUT?
?!
IT GOT BETTER!
HUH ?!
...EXCEPT HIM. HE TOOK YOU SERIOUSLY.
HE SEEMED, I DUNNO, DIFFERENT FROM ALL THE OTHER GUYS.
STILL, THAT GUY YOU WERE TALKING TO...
HOW?!
JUST ABOUT EVERYBODY HERE HAS TOTALLY BLOWN US OFF...
北川第一
2

...?
THE FIRST ROUND ...
THE SECOND ROUND ...
MY TEAM'S GONNA WIN.
AND KEEP WIN-NING.
WE'RE GONNA WIN AND WIN AND PLAY A TON OF GAMES!
FINALLY ...
I FINALLY HAVE SIX PEOPLE TOGETHER. I CAN FINALLY PLAY A REAL GAME ON A REAL COURT!
...
YOU'LL LEARN THAT IN OUR MATCH.
ENOUGH TO MAKE UP FOR ALL THE ONES I COULDN'T PLAY BEFORE.
...
北川第一
中学校
バレーボール部
DOOM
IN THE FIRST ROUND ...
AND THE SECOND ROUND ...
AND THE FINALS...
AND ALL THE WAY UP TO THE NATIONALS!
WHRL

HAH! YOU SAY THAT LIKE IT'S EASY.
THIS IS VOLLEYBALL.
DO YOU EVEN UNDERSTAND HOW CRITICAL HEIGHT IS TO THIS SPORT?
!
I KNOW I'M NOT VERY TALL ...
BUT THAT DOESN'T MATTER!
I...
...CAN FLY!!
THERE'S NO SUCH THING AS A MATCH THAT'S DECIDED BEFORE IT EVEN STARTS.
...
AS LONG AS YOU DON'T GIVE UP--
NOT GIVING UP IS EASIER SAID THAN DONE.
SOME GUTS AND A STUBBORN STREAK ...
...AREN'T ENOUGH TO MAKE UP FOR SKILL, SIZE AND TALENT.
...

QUIT SLINGING THE SCHOOL'S REP AROUND LIKE IT'S YOUR OWN.
...AND YOU THINK YOU'RE GOOD ENOUGH TO TALK SMACK ABOUT OUR OPPONENT?
NONE OF YOU EVEN MANAGED TO EARN A SPOT ON THE BENCH...
YOU THREE.
URK

URK!
GLORG
GURGL
I WAS JUST ABOUT TO TELL THEM OFF TOO!
AH
DARN! I CAN'T LET HIM TAKE CONTROL!
W-WELL...
YEEP!!
S-S-SORRY!!
DASH

!!

I'M HERE TO WIN!!

GUYS WHO DON'T WATCH THEIR HEALTH SHOULDN'T TALK BIG EITHER!
THAT'S WHY YOU GET MADE FUN OF.
H-HEY!!
GLUGL GLRGL GLUURG
IT'S COMMON SENSE TO MAKE SURE YOU'RE COMPLETELY PREPARED FOR EVERYTHING BEFORE A TOURNAMENT.
SO YOU CAN HAVE SOME FUN MEMORIES OF YOUR LAST YEAR?
WHY ARE YOU EVEN HERE?

OFFICIAL WARM-UPS ARE STARTING.
GET YOUR BUTTS MOVING.
TOBIO KAGEYAMA
KITAGAWA DAIICHI MIDDLE SCHOOL
3RD YEAR
北川第一中学校
バレーボール部
!!
...
SORRY. WE'LL FINISH UP RIGHT NOW.
CRAP! IT'S KAGEYAMA-SAN!
GLANCE
...
HEY!!
HA HA HA! YOU'VE GOT A POINT, MAN!
YEAH, BUT ARE WE REALLY GONNA NEED THAT MUCH? ESPECIALLY AGAINST THEM!
HUH ?!
HURRY UP! WE'VE GOTTA FILL TWO MORE BOTTLES.
TMD

JOLT
HEY, YOU!! DON'T COUNT US OUT YET!!
NAH, THEY'RE ALL FIRST YEARS.
HECK, HALF OF THEM LOOK LIKE ELEMENTARY KIDS!
THEY DON'T EVEN HAVE A LIBERO!
YEAH! DID YOU SEE HOW FEW OF THEM THERE ARE?
CLOSE ENOUGH! HOW THE HECK DO THEY THINK THEY CAN STAND UP TO US?
POK
北川第一
HEY.
WE'RE UP AGAINST WHO, NOW? YUKIGAOKA MIDDLE SCHOOL? NEVER HEARD OF 'EM.
YOU'D BETTER BE READY! ULP...! A...AS SOON AS MY GUT...ULG! FEELS BETTER... I'MMA GO OUT ON THAT COURT AND THRASH YOU-- GOO...
GURRGL
URRRRG...
...
W.C
YO, SECOND YEARS.
THEY'RE MAKING FUN OF ME!
RRRGH!
GURGL
ANNA, DOES YOUR TUMMY HURT?
OH, REALLY! WE'LL LOOK FORWARD TO IT!
YOU IDIOT, LOOK! HE'S GOT THE CAPTAIN PATCH! HE'S THEIR CAPTAIN!
SEE! HE'S AN ELEMENTARY KID!
BFFTAHA HA HA!

WHRL
B-B-BUT... WHAT DO I USUALLY TALK ABOUT, AGAIN?
GET IT TO-GETHER, MAN!!
GRP
?!
WHAT THE HECK?!
KITA ICHI !!
BAM!
VICTORY! KITAGAWA DAIICHI MIDDLE SCHOOL

THEY'RE HUGE!!
THEY'RE SCARY !!
...!!
GOOONG

KITA ICHI !!
BAM!
DUN
北川第一

AGAIN ?!
BUT I GOTTA GO TO THE BATHROOM FIRST...
GURGLE

MURMUR
MURMUR
MURMUR

YEAH!
THAT'S RIGHT. YOU CAN JUMP SURPRISINGLY HIGH, SHO-CHAN.
GRP
FOR ONCE, YOU ACTUALLY LOOK RELIABLE !
...I'LL JUMP UP AND SPIKE THE BALL RIGHT OVER 'EM!!
I HAVE COMPLETE FAITH IN MY JUMPING SKILLS! IT DOESN'T MATTER HOW TALL THE OTHER TEAM IS...

THEY'RE OUR OPPONENTS?! ARE THEY REALLY MIDDLE SCHOOLERS?!
THE HECK ?!
TKOMF
R-RELAX! WE'LL BE FINE!

GLARE
FLINCH
?!
?
WHAT THE HECK?! GEEZ, THAT WAS SCARY!
WHRL
I DON'T KNOW HOW HE WOUND UP WITH THE NICKNAME, BUT...
SO WHAT'S UP WITH THAT KING GUY?
TMP
TMP
TMP
TMP
TMP
TMP
"THE KING OF THE COURT," TOBIO KAGEYAMA!
...HE'S SUPPOSED TO BE REALLY GOOD.
HE'S GOT GREAT INSTINCTS FOR THE GAME AND IS A MONSTER SETTER. HE'S AN ELITE ON-COURT LEADER.
WOW.
I CAN UNDERSTAND BEING NERVOUS THOUGH.
HUH?!
YOU BEING QUIET MAKES ME UNEASY!!
SHOYO, DON'T CLAM UP!!
BUMP BUMP
URK
TMP
TMP
PWEEET
SWFF
SWFF
ISN'T IT ALMOST TIME, SHO-CHAN?
UH... YEAH...
HUH?
雪ケ丘
1

YAMMER YAMMER
!
SPEAK OF THE DEVIL...
HERE THEY COME.
THERE'S YUKIGAOKA MIDDLE SCHOOL.
THE POOR SCRUBS THAT HAVE TO GO UP AGAINST KITAGAWA DAIICHI RIGHT OFF THE BAT.
A BUNCH OF NOBODIES GOING UP AGAINST A TITLE CONTENDER IN ROUND ONE? SO UNLUCKY!
雪ヶ丘
*JERSEY: YUKIGAOKA
TMP
IT'S KITAGAWA DAIICHI!
北川第一 中学校 バレーボール部
*JACKET: KITAGAWA DAIICHI MIDDLE SCHOOL VOLLEYBALL CLUB
THAT'S HIM! IT'S GOTTA BE!
YOU KNOW...
AH!
LOOK!
TROMP
WHOA, THEY'RE HUGE!
TALK ABOUT INTIMIDATING!

HUH? WE'RE A COBBLED-TOGETHER TEAM OF TOTAL ROOKIES, AND YOU THINK WE'LL WIN?
DUH! COURSE I DO!
...
WE'VE FINALLY MADE IT INTO A TOURNAMENT.
AND NOW THAT WE'RE IN IT... WE'RE GONNA WIN IT!
MURMUR
IZUMIN. KOJI.
MURMUR
WHERE DOES HE GET ALL THAT OPTIMISM?
IT MEANS A LOT TO ME.
!!
THANKS FOR BEING HERE TODAY.
SAYS THE GUY WITH TEARS IN HIS EYES.
I'M NOT CRYING!
GAWD, SHOYO! QUIT CRYIN'!
THEM WHO?
LOOK. OVER THERE. THAT'S THEM.
AH HA HA... WELL, WE DID LOSE OUR OWN TOURNAMENTS ALREADY.
QUIT IT! YOU'RE EMBARRASSING ME!
UM! Y-YOU'RE WELCOME, CAPTAIN. BUT WE'RE STILL TOTAL ROOKIES...
AND THE MIRACLE FIRST YEARS! THREE OF YOU EVEN! THANK YOU FOR JOINING! THANK YOU SO MUCH!!
HUG

SMELL ALL THAT ICY HOT SPRAY!!
GRP
SHOYO HINATA
YUKIGAOKA MIDDLE SCHOOL
3RD YEAR
VOLLEYBALL CLUB CAPTAIN
YEAH. HE REALLY HUNG IN THERE ALL BY HIMSELF.
NO KIDDING. I'M SHOCKED HE ACTUALLY MADE IT THIS FAR. DIDN'T HE START AS THE ONLY TEAM MEMBER?
MY THIRD YEAR, AND I FINALLY... FINALLY ...!!
KNEEN
H-HEY! I CAN'T HELP IT! THIS IS MY FIRST REAL TOURNAMENT!
DOES SOMEBODY HAVE STAGE FRIGHT, HMM?
GEEZ, SHO-CHAN. NERVOUS MUCH?
"Smell the Icy Hot spray"? Seriously?
I...I KNOW!
IT'S NOT LIKE YOU GAVE US MUCH NOTICE FOR THIS! WE BARELY KNOW ANY OF THE RULES!
YEAH!
HE'S RIGHT, CAPTAIN. DON'T YOU HAVE A JOB TO DO?
UM, CAPTAIN? SHOULDN'T WE WARM UP?
KOJI SEKIMUKAI
3RD YEAR
(ACTUALLY IN THE SOCCER CLUB)
YUKITAKA IZUMI
3RD YEAR
(ACTUALLY IN THE BASKETBALL CLUB)
TWITCH
TWITCH
TWITCH
VOLLEYBALL CLUB 1ST YEARS
MORI
KAWASHIMA
SUZUKI

BA TA M!

ROUGHLY THREE YEARS AND THREE MONTHS LATER...

*JERSEY: KOUSEN ACADEMY

HE'S LIKE A LITTLE GIANT!!
Panasunic
MISAKA ELECTRONICS
...IS WHAT I HEARD THE ANNOUNCER SHOUT OVER THE TV.
CONGRATS! KARASUNO GOES TO THE SPRING TOURNEY!
THAT...
MARKET
I CLEARLY REMEMBER STANDING THERE, WATCHING ...
...SHIVERING IN AWE AS THE LITTLE BLACK-CLAD ATHLETE...
...SCORED POINT AFTER POINT.
...QUALIFIED FOR THE NATIONAL HIGH SCHOOL SPRING VOLLEYBALL TOURNAMENT.
KARASUNO HIGH SCHOOL, IN THE NEXT TOWN OVER FROM MINE...
*JERSEY: KARASUNO
...THERE STOOD A SINGLE ATHLETE AT A MERE 5'7" TALL.
ON A COURT FILLED WITH PLAYERS TOWERING OVER 6 FEET TALL...

HAIKYU!!

CHAPTER 1: Endings and Beginnings

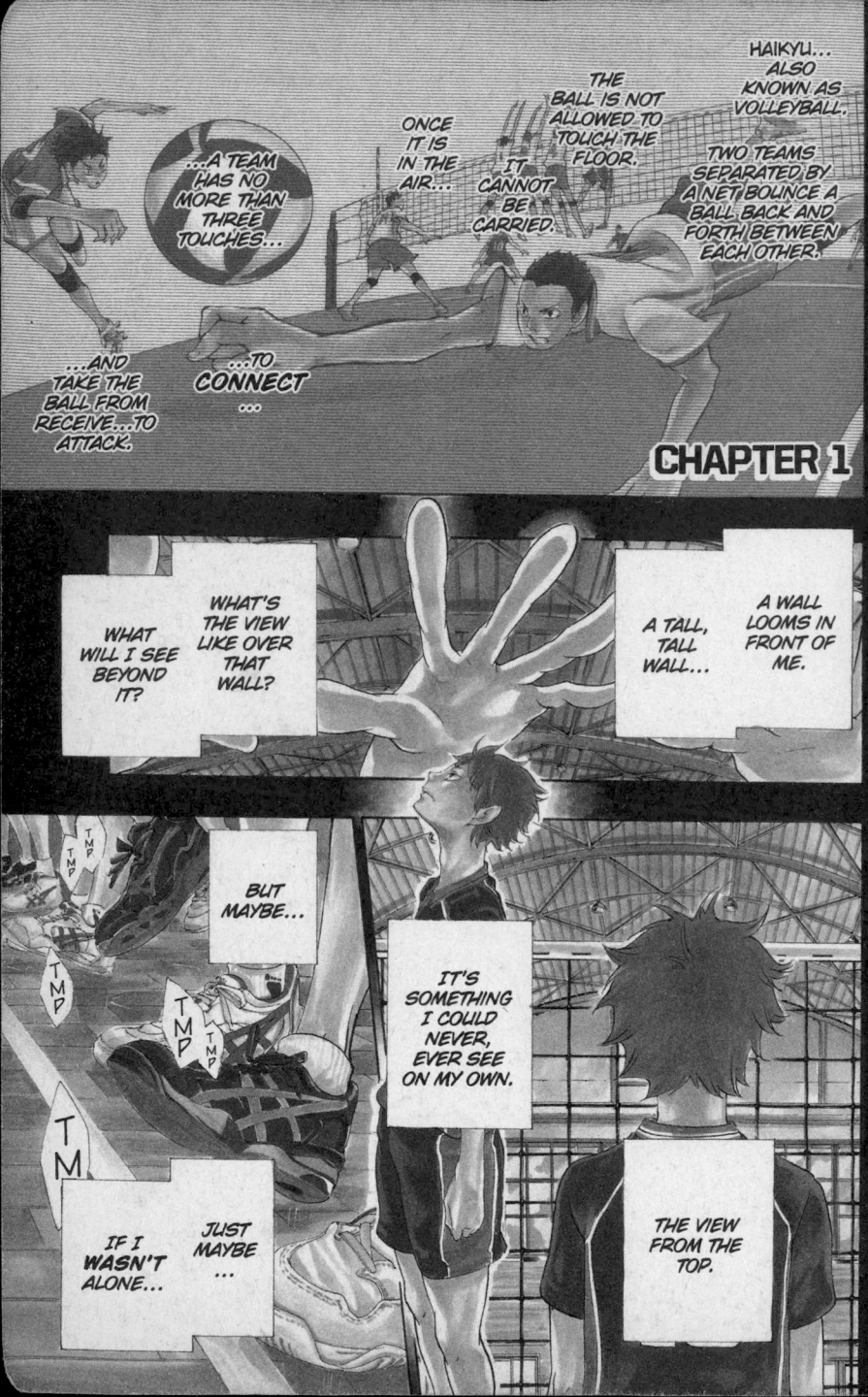
HAIKYU... ALSO KNOWN AS VOLLEYBALL.
TWO TEAMS SEPARATED BY A NET BOUNCE A BALL BACK AND FORTH BETWEEN EACH OTHER.
THE BALL IS NOT ALLOWED TO TOUCH THE FLOOR.
IT CANNOT BE CARRIED.
ONCE IT IS IN THE AIR...
...A TEAM HAS NO MORE THAN THREE TOUCHES...
...TO CONNECT ...
...AND TAKE THE BALL FROM RECEIVE...TO ATTACK.
CHAPTER 1
A WALL LOOMS IN FRONT OF ME.
A TALL, TALL WALL...
WHAT'S THE VIEW LIKE OVER THAT WALL?
WHAT WILL I SEE BEYOND IT?
THE VIEW FROM THE TOP.
IT'S SOMETHING I COULD NEVER, EVER SEE ON MY OWN.
JUST MAYBE ...
IF I WASN'T ALONE...
BUT MAYBE...
TMP
TMP
TMP
TMP
TMP
TMP
TM

1 HINATA AND KAGEYAMA

CHAPTER 1:
Endings and Beginnings 005

CHAPTER 2:
Karasuno High School Volleyball Club 061

CHAPTER 3:
Single-Celled Organisms 087

CHAPTER 4:
The Greatest Teammate 111

CHAPTER 5:
The King of the Court 131

CHAPTER 6:
Middle School Story 151

CHAPTER 7:
Words from the Have-Nots 171

SHONENJUMP MANGA

HARUICHI FURUDATE

HINATA AND KAGEYAMA 1

HAIKYU!!

VOLUME 1

SHONEN JUMP Manga Edition

Story and Art by
HARUICHI FURUDATE

Translation 1 **ADRIENNE BECK**
Touch-Up Art & Lettering 2 **ERIKA TERRIQUEZ**
Design 3 **FAWN LAU**
Editor 4 **MARLENE FIRST**

HAIKYU!! © 2012 by Haruichi Furudate
All rights reserved.
First published in Japan in 2012 by SHUEISHA Inc., Tokyo.
English translation rights arranged by SHUEISHA Inc.

The stories, characters and incidents mentioned in this publication are entirely fictional.

No portion of this book may be reproduced or transmitted in any form or by any means without written permission from the copyright holders.

Printed in the U.S.A.

Published by VIZ Media, LLC
P.O. Box 77010
San Francisco, CA 94107

10 9 8 7 6 5 4 3 2 1
First printing, July 2016

www.shonenjump.com

www.viz.com

Thank you for picking up *Haikyu!!* volume 1! I hope you like it. For those of you who are like, "Volleyball? Never played it. I don't even know the rules!" ...I hope to make this a story full of fun and great characters you'll enjoy and who will make you want to say, "I want to root for these guys!"

HARUICHI FURUDATE began his manga career when he was 25 years old with the one-shot *Ousama Kid* (King Kid), which won an honorable mention for the 14th Jump Treasure Newcomer Manga Prize. His first series, *Kiben Gakuha, Yotsuya Sensei no Kaidan* (Philosophy School, Yotsuya Sensei's Ghost Stories), was serialized in Weekly Shonen Jump in 2010. In 2012, he began serializing *Haikyu!!* in Weekly Shonen Jump, where it became his most popular work to date.